THE ANATOMY OF THE FLOOR

By Leonard Sloane

THE GREAT MERCHANTS
(with Tom Mahoney)
THE ANATOMY OF THE FLOOR

Leonard Sloane

THE ANATOMY OF THE FLOOR

---

*The Trillion-dollar Market
at the New York Stock Exchange*

DOUBLEDAY & COMPANY, INC.

GARDEN CITY, NEW YORK

1980

ISBN: 0-385-12249-7
Library of Congress Catalog Card Number 77–15173
Copyright © 1980 by LEONARD SLOANE

First Edition

For Annette, Elliot, and Steven

ACKNOWLEDGMENTS

This book was written after conducting dozens of interviews with past and present members, officials, and employees of the New York Stock Exchange, reading hundreds of thousands of words that others have written about it, and spending hundreds of hours at my typewriter preparing the manuscript. I was generously assisted by many people who offered information, opinions, and criticism and to whom I will be eternally grateful. But whatever flaws, inferences, and conclusions exist in this work are mine alone.

My thanks must go first to the Exchange, which arranged a number of interviews with key figures in this book and gave me access to its historical clippings scrapbooks. I have not attempted to write an official history, and the Exchange is in no way responsible for anything included herein. I especially appreciate, however, the cooperation given by William M. Batten, chairman and chief executive officer of the NYSE; John J. Phelan, Jr., a vice-chairman; and Robert C. Hall, former executive vice-president. Many of the people on the Exchange staff were also helpful, and I would particularly like to acknowledge two former staffers, Richard Callanan and Edward DeLaura, whose encyclopedic knowledge of Exchange lore was invaluable. Charles D. Storer, assistant vice-president for public information, Philip J. Keuper, former vice-president for communications, and George B. Bookman, a consultant to the Exchange, were kind enough to explain policies and procedures and to provide current and historical background material.

All of the paid heads of the New York Stock Exchange in the twentieth century gave generously of their time to share with me some of their thoughts about events and attitudes during their tenure at the Big Board. The presidents and chairmen who made themselves available to me at different times during my research were William McChesney Martin, Jr.; Emil Schram; G. Keith Funston; Robert W. Haack; James J. Needham; and William M. Batten.

So many members of the Exchange were interviewed during the course of assembling this book that individual acknowledgments run the risk of forgetting some names. Two members went far out of their way to open doors for me: Bernard J. Lasker of Lasker, Stone & Stern, who gave me counsel and direction at the inception of the book, and George H. Rose of Lazard Frères & Co., who introduced me to a large number of other members and who is, I discovered, a man of many talents.

Other members of the Big Board whom I would like to acknowledge include Elmer M. Bloch; George C. Dinsmore; Walter N. Frank; Leonard Wagner; Donald B. Stott; Henry M. Watts, Jr.; David Granger; Donald Stone; James Crane Kellogg III; Herbert J. McCooey; George Willett; Thomas Schwalenberg; Thomas F. Jessop; Gerard Meyer; Harry M. Jacobson; and R. Peter Rose. Donald T.

Regan of Merrill Lynch, Pierce, Fenner & Smith; James W. Davant of Paine, Webber, Jackson & Curtis; Harry A. Jacobs, Jr., of Bache Halsey Stuart Shields; Sanford I. Weill of Shearson Loeb Rhoades; and Robert M. Gardiner of Dean Witter Reynolds Corporation are among the senior executives of securities firms who offered invaluable insights into the workings of the stock market.

Two friends, Alan W. Leeds and Robert L. Leeds, Jr., told me about their father, Robert L. Leeds, who made $25,000 by buying and selling a Big Board seat within less than two months early in 1929. Jack Bronston, Gerald Casper, Jaromir Ledecky, Werner Levy, Sandy Lewis, Tom Mahoney, David Rachman, Robert E. Rubin, David Shechet, and Sherman Simanowitz are others whose friendship and assistance during the preparation of this book are deeply appreciated.

Muriel F. Siebert, the first woman member of the New York Stock Exchange and now the New York State Superintendent of Banks, gave me some of my initial interviews for the book and led me in new directions that turned out to be most useful. In Washington, Harold M. Williams, chairman of the Securities and Exchange Commission; his predecessor, Roderick Hills; and other commissioners and staff members at the SEC freely discussed their views about activities on the floor of the Big Board. On Capitol Hill, two congressmen who played a large role in the development of recent securities legislation—Senator Harrison A. Williams, Jr., of New Jersey and former Representative John E. Moss of California—spoke frankly about Wall Street as seen from the nation's capital.

I also wish to express my gratitude to John M. Lee, the financial-business editor of the New York *Times*, for his encouragement and support during the years that this book was in preparation. In addition, I am thankful to the late Thomas E. Mullaney, the former financial-business editor of the *Times*, whose guidance and enthusiasm were munificent when this book was conceived.

Julian Bach, my agent, and Stewart Richardson, Associate Publisher of Doubleday & Company, were instrumental in formulating the thesis and approach of this book. From the beginning, they not only were supportive, but also demonstrated a broad understanding of the New York Stock Exchange and its members.

Finally I must publicly state what I have expressed privately on many occasions: this book could never have been completed without the continued love and support provided by my wife, Annette, and my sons, Elliot and Steven. Their words spurred me on when spurring was needed, and their advice on matters practical and theoretical often proved to be enormously valuable. The dedication, therefore, is to them for very good reason.

LEONARD SLOANE
September 1979

CONTENTS

Part IV
The Floor in Action

Part V
The Floor of Tomorrow

PART I

Who's Who on the New York Stock Exchange

1 THE MEMBERS

The floor of the New York Stock Exchange is first and foremost a place of business. Hundreds of millions of dollars' worth of stocks and bonds are bought and sold there every working day by brokers, acting for their customers or for themselves. As the value of these securities rise and fall, the worth of major corporations, the holdings of huge financial institutions, and the personal resources of the people on the trading floor rise and fall too. Perhaps most important, some 25 million American investors are directly affected by what happens in the big, ground-level, paper-littered rooms of this impressive granite building with its Corinthian columns at the corner of Broad and Wall streets in New York City, while the other 200 million or so are indirectly affected.

For the ornate floor—actually three immense rooms with marble walls and a gold ceiling—is the marketplace where buyers and sellers come together to trade the securities of the leading companies of American industry. The basic natural resources, the major manufacturers, the great utilities, the transportation networks, and the leading service businesses in the United States are all publicly owned and have their shares listed on the New York exchange. Called the Big Board by both proponents and detractors, it is the largest securities exchange in the nation, with some fifteen hundred and fifty corporations listed and an annual volume of more than 7 billion shares, representing 80 percent of all trading on United States exchanges. The eyes of the financial world are riveted on its ticker tape, whose symbols and numbers flash electronically across thousands of screens in boardrooms and offices throughout the nation six hours a day. And the floor of the Exchange is the nerve center of the financial world, where securities professionals buy and sell millions of shares worth millions of dollars every one of these days.

But the floor is more than a marketplace for investors and speculators. It is the home for 1,366 members of the New York Stock Exchange who have purchased "seats," plus a handful who have bought annual memberships, giving them the right to be there and trade with their peers. Nonmembers, institutions as well as individuals, who wish to buy and sell securities on the Exchange must do so through a member—and pay him accordingly. Whatever monopolistic rights these members had to do business in stocks listed on the New York exchange have been breaking down slowly in recent years with the gradual development of a national market system for trading securities. But the designation printed on letterheads, doorways, and advertisements of "Member of the New York Stock Exchange" still means prestige, power, and, usually, wealth.

Not every member of the Exchange spends full time on the floor. Some of those who have acquired seats are "upstairs" members—executives of brokerage firms who work in their offices, not only in New York, but throughout the country as well. Some of these upstairs members, moreover, are the only people in their firms who own a Big

Board membership and have spent anywhere from the all-time high price of $515,000 (1968 and 1969) to the twentieth-century low price of $17,000 (1942) for the right to put the New York Stock Exchange membership designation on their door. Yet while these upstairs members are connected with firms with enormous assets and instant public recognition, even they recognize that the floor is the real focus around which the Exchange revolves.

Without the floor, there would be no Exchange—no administration, no upstairs members, no subsidiary organizations, and no satellite companies that exist in the Wall Street area because, like Mount Everest, the floor is there. The main function of the Exchange is to serve as an auction medium for trading securities, and the floor is the place where this trading is done. Although detractors talk, sometimes wistfully, sometimes antagonistically, about an electronic "black box" in New Jersey or Cincinnati replacing the entire apparatus of the New York exchange, the floor seems likely to continue to function in one shape or another for many years to come.

And with the floor come its members: vigorous, shrewd, mischievous, clannish, sophisticated, speculative, and, above all, protective of their hard-won rights. Floor members will fight vigorously against other members all day long to make one eighth of a point (12½ cents) on a trade, whether it is for 100 shares or 10,000 shares. But when the outside world—in the form of a congressperson, a regulator, a newspaper reporter, or any other nonmember—attacks the floor, its members join together in a brotherhood of business that plans its moves so cleverly and wields its power so forcefully that for decade upon decade it has been virtually unbeatable.

In 1976 and 1977, for example, an attempt was made by the administration of the Exchange, acting through a committee appointed by its board of directors, to enlarge access to the floor by allowing nonmembers to "rent" seats instead of buying them. This proposal to allow for the sale of physical-access and electronic memberships by the Exchange, on a yearly basis, met with such a torrent of opposition and abuse from floor members that the power structure was caught completely unaware. At one Exchange meeting, these members shouted their opposition to any additional, short-term members so vigorously that it took enormous pressure by the board of directors and those that supported them to put the access proposal—long demanded to one extent or another by Congress and the Securities and Exchange Commission (SEC)—through to an affirmative vote. Even so, the membership, led by those on the floor, voted in 1979 to reverse themselves and restrict outsiders from buying yearly access to the Exchange without purchasing a seat.

Floor members like to think of themselves as a breed apart, as many who know them will agree. From the earliest days of the Exchange almost two centuries ago, these men have risked their own capital as they matched wits with their peers to choose winning securities for their clients and themselves. Many have come to the floor as poor boys and left as rich men—although the opposite is not unknown in floor lore, either.

At the top rung of the ladder on which floor members position themselves are the specialists, also known as brokers' brokers. These men—and there are still only men in this role, although the Exchange constitution no longer provides for an all-male membership—fulfill two roles: holding in their books limit orders that are left with them by brokers for execution when the market price reaches the price of the order, and acting as a principal for their own accounts. In the first situation they are simply agents, while in the second they serve as dealers, buying and selling with the stated obligation of maintaining fair and orderly continuous markets in the stocks assigned to them. Their basic function is to give liquidity to the marketplace so that investors can buy and sell securities on better terms than they might otherwise with less supply and demand. Not so incidentally, specialists are handsomely rewarded for doing so.

There are 392 specialists registered on the New York Stock Exchange, and their incomes often reach the stratospheric level. Some of them earn $400,000, $500,000, or more each year, while earnings of at least $100,000 are not uncommon. Even the youngest and newest specialists, who are usually lent the money by the firm in which they become a partner or stockholder to purchase their seats, find themselves almost immediately at the $50,000-a-year level, with the opportunity to move up quickly to still-higher amounts.

A second category of membership is the commission broker, a person affiliated with a Big Board member organization that does business with the public. These brokers—there are now a few women who work along with the male commission brokers on the floor, to make a total of 611—execute the buy and sell orders that are sent to them by their firms via telephone or Teletype. Their compensation is usually a percentage of the firm's commission rate, which had been a fixed fee until 1975, when fully negotiated commissions were imposed on the securities business by the Securities and Exchange Commission.

Next in the pecking order come the independent floor

brokers, who handle orders for firms whose commission brokers may be unavailable or whose policy is to have no members on the floor. The 196 members of this group are also called two-dollar brokers, because at one time their fee was two dollars for every one hundred shares of stock executed. Today they receive substantially more, but their role has become less vital to the functioning of the floor with electronic systems taking over much of their historic role.

There are also 73 competitive traders operating for their own accounts on the floor, buying and selling stock without paying any commissions in an effort to make a profit on their knowledge of the market. Working under special rules that limit their ability to transact business under certain conditions, these traders also provide more opportunities for investors and speculators off the floor to trade at prices close to the previous selling price.

Finally, there are 54 registered competitive market makers, who act like competitive traders but who also have particular obligations imposed on them by the Big Board. When called upon, they must make a bid or offer that will narrow the existing quote spread or improve the depth of an existing quote.

Some of the floor professionals, like traders or market makers, fit into more than one of these membership categories, and the total of the individual classifications therefore does not add up to 1,366.

In addition to these seat holders, there are another thousand or so employees of both the member firms and the Exchange who spend all of their working hours on the floor: clerks, pages, supervisors, and others. With a total of more than 2,500 people on a five-story-high, 16,000-square-foot trading floor filled with specialists' posts and brokers' booths, a buzz of excitement normally pervades the area during the day. And when trading accelerates because of an important news announcement or a sudden market development, the noise grows steadily louder until it sometimes erupts into a roar.

It is during these hectic periods that the skills and techniques of the floor members come into the sharpest play. For that is when the commission brokers must negotiate the hardest for the best price, when specialists must watch the level of orders in their books with the most care, and when traders must look the most carefully for buy and sell openings. The great operators on the floor of the present day, as well as those who made their mark in the past, have been at their best in active markets when the ticker tape moved at peak speed and prices advanced or fell in rapid spurts.

A reason for this rise in the adrenaline of those on the floor during the most crucial trading periods is the strong sense of the gambler within them. With all of the federal and New York Stock Exchange regulatory emphasis on the safeguards of investing, those on the floor know that they have to take a chance to make a buck. Some floor brokers will trade in and out of a single stock all day long at one eighth of a point difference per trade. By doing nothing more than this, some can earn $100, $200, or more daily after expenses. Those who consistently put their money on the wrong side of an order soon find themselves off the floor and in another field of endeavor.

But those who are more often right than wrong find themselves in a lifetime occupation with enormous rewards, both economic and psychological. Not only do members of the Exchange take home huge incomes in the form of salaries and return on investments, but they also have a tremendous impact on the entire society by virtue of their positions. When these members set in motion changes that result in greater securities trading or sharp fluctuations in the value of the traded securities, it is not just the individuals and institutions that own stocks and bonds who realize the effect. Workers, farmers, housewives, students, and just about everyone else react to these changes through their paychecks, their sales to others, and their standards of living.

The last few years have seen movements on a number of fronts to dissipate the power long held by members of the Exchange. The greatest impetus has come from Washington, where Congress and the SEC have been suggesting, prodding, and finally demanding the creation of a national market system. The establishment of such a system—electronically linking the New York Stock Exchange, the regional securities exchanges, the over-the-counter market, and the "third market" of off-board trading by institutional investors in NYSE stocks—would obviously loosen the grip of the Big Board over the most significant securities trading in the nation. As this system evolves, moreover, the confusion that naturally surrounds any new development is a serious problem for the Exchange administration and members to overcome.

Still another problem facing the New York Stock Exchange is the recent revitalization of the other securities exchanges, including the American Stock Exchange in New York City and the Boston, Philadelphia, Midwest, and Pacific exchanges in other cities. Until about a decade ago regional exchanges were relatively insignificant compared with the Big Board and based the prices of their trades almost exclusively on New York Stock Exchange orders. But with these exchanges obtaining a larger share of the overall volume, their plunge into new developments like options long before the New York exchange took any action, and the growth of competitive market making in the most widely traded stocks, the regionals have become a much more potent factor that the Big Board must now consider rather than ignore.

Despite its flaws, and because of the record of its floor members in stabilizing what might otherwise have been erratic price movements and in providing what is probably the best auction market for securities in the world, the New York exchange is still in place, functioning as a major component of the capital-formation mechanism for American industry. And perhaps belatedly, it is also reacting to the forces that gathered against it during the 1960s and 1970s with new products and programs of its own. The Big Board announced a plan in 1976 to trade options in its stocks, a process that other exchanges began as early as four years previously, but action has been held up for many years because of an SEC moratorium. It has proposed a method of linking the exchanges in a central market whereby it would not lose its identity, and has not only won most of the other exchanges over to this point of view but also taken the initial steps toward implementation. It is developing a more open stance to the public regarding its operations, its finances, and its goals in order to win friends and influence people. And it has created a separate futures exchange to trade in the rapidly growing financial instruments.

As a result of these actions, the New York Stock Exchange, which is coming close to the bicentennial of its founding, can look ahead to even further expansion from its current status as a trillion-dollar marketplace. Its floor, in whatever form and in whatever location, is likely to continue as the most meaningful place in the world for trading securities, even if others will provide more competition for this historic role than they have in the past. And its floor members—who have, more than any other group, made the Exchange what it was and what it is—will undoubtedly continue to develop new ways of coping with the changing times as they strive to maintain an effective, functional organization for the years ahead.

PART II

From Yesterday
to Today

2

THE
BUTTONWOOD TREE
AND ALL THAT

The floor of the New York Stock Exchange that its modern-day denizens occupy bears scant resemblance to the tiny exchange that was created in 1792 for the purchase and sale of stock in lower Manhattan. Yet today's Big Board is a direct descendant of the organization that was formed that year, when a group of brokers met under a buttonwood tree in front of 68 Wall Street and formalized their trading arrangements.

The era during which the Exchange was formed was the era in which the new nation called the United States of America took shape. New York City was then the nation's capital, and the first Congress convened on the site of what is now Federal Hall, across Broad Street from the present location of the Exchange at 11 Wall Street. It was at that time also that the first Secretary of the Treasury, Alexander Hamilton, convinced Congress to consolidate the Revolutionary War debt authorized by the Continental Congress by issuing $80 million in government bonds, which were then called stock.

This stock was very much in demand and was traded in New York's financial district—then as now in the Wall Street area—first in offices and coffee houses and then in auction rooms. A pattern developed whereby, at noontime, five independent auctioneers ran a public stock exchange in rotation at their places of business at the eastern end of Wall Street. Investors began using brokers to buy and sell for them at these auctions, and before long the brokers and the auctioneers became bitter rivals for dominance in the fledgling stock market.

Buying and selling were so much in the air that in 1791 James Madison wrote to Thomas Jefferson that "stocks and scrip [of the First Bank of the United States, forerunner of the Federal Reserve Banks] are the sole domestic subjects of conversation . . . speculations . . . carried on with money borrowed at from 2½ per cent a month to 1 per cent a week."

By 1792 brokers began to meet outdoors on non-rainy days to trade on their own without auctioneers, congregating in front of a buttonwood, or sycamore, tree on Wall Street. Stock trading was only a small portion of their business, since they also traded commodities, handled commercial factoring, and were even in the insurance and banking business. Competition was strong and ethical practices were as much the exception as the rule.

In the spring of that year, as competition with the auctioneers intensified, a group of the stockbrokers met at Corre's Hotel and agreed not to attend any public auction sale of stocks. Soon thereafter, on May 17, 1792, the Buttonwood Agreement was formally signed, establishing a guild of brokers and, in effect, creating an organization that would eventually become the New York Stock Exchange. This agreement among twenty-one individuals and three partnerships moreover set the pattern for dealings on the exchange until recent years, with these words:

> We, the subscribers, brokers for the purchase and
> sale of public stocks, do hereby solemnly promise and

pledge ourselves to each other that we will not buy or sell from this date, for any person whatsoever, any kind of public stocks at a rate less than one-quarter of one per cent commission on the specie value, and that we will give preference to each other in our negotiations.

The signers of the Buttonwood Agreement met regularly under the buttonwood tree to trade in the securities that were then popular among investors: government bonds, shares of insurance companies, the First Bank of the United States, the Bank of North America, and the Bank of New York. They quickly captured the bulk of the trades from the auctioneers and went on to develop into a permanent grouping that became more powerful with each passing month.

As their strength as an institution grew, the buttonwood brokers decided that they needed an indoor, as well as an outdoor, meeting place, and so they built a building on the northwest corner of Wall and William streets in the winter of 1793. This building—called the Tontine Coffee House after a seventeenth-century Italian banker who gave his name to a type of financial arrangement—was used as both a club and a meeting room, serving the business and social needs of its members. At this time, memberships also began to be known as seats, since members sat in the coffee house and transacted their business there. Even after they moved indoors, the stockbrokers continued to make most of their money in other activities and the Tontine's business reputation was far less than its members hoped it would be. Some of the most ethical members, in fact, would remain only for the stock auctions, while those who hung around the building would attempt to get involved with other deals by betting each other on a wide range of categories. One of these members was John Jacob Astor, the founder of the Astor dynasty, who began his American career with seven flutes his brother had made in London and wound up at his death with more than $25 million.

In the first quarter century of its existence the organization formed by the buttonwood brokers kept itself going despite a low level of trading. With little investment capital available, an immature banking system, the passing of political power from the Federalists to the Republicans, and the disruption of commerce and trade by the War of 1812, trading in securities was at best an erratic activity. Furthermore, the United States was still an agricultural rather than an industrial society, and the concept of limited liability for owners of stock in corporations had not yet taken hold. Not only was distrust in government strong, but small entrepreneurs were not anxious to invest the profits from their own businesses in distant corporations. And brokers in Philadelphia and Boston were considered more substantial individuals for the formidable task of investing funds than the group that had signed the Buttonwood Agreement in New York.

Shortly after the War of 1812, however, the New York brokers—as well as the stock market itself—started to expand in scope. The federal government undertook a policy of encouraging financial expansion, and new businesses spurted up all over the country. Banks, insurance companies, cotton mills, and canals were the nation's growth industries at the time. As speculation grew, brokers in New York and Philadelphia vied with each other for the right to sell shares in the newly prospering companies.

A formal stock exchange had first been established in Philadelphia in 1754, and what has since become the Philadelphia Stock Exchange was officially founded in 1790. Because of its organization, efficiency, and self-regulatory powers, the Philadelphia exchange drew substantial amounts of business away from New York, particularly purchases and sales made by European investors. And so the New York brokers realized that they would have to develop a more traditional business arrangement to govern their trading activities.

After sending a representative to Philadelphia to study its method of operation, the New York group drew up a similarly worded constitution in 1817 for an organization called the New York Stock and Exchange Board. The first paid president of this Board, a broker named Anthony Stockholm, was in charge of the auction, which began every morning at 11:30 A.M. At that time the exchange functioned as a call, rather than a continuous, market, with the names of the stocks called out in turn and bids and offers made by the twenty-eight individual member brokers. All contracts had to be settled by 2:15 the following afternoon, a procedure that remained in effect for more than one hundred years.

Among the rules of the organization was the blackball, whereby three negative votes could exclude a person from membership. Wash sales—fictitious sales from one broker to another to give the impression of activity in a stock—were forbidden. And fines ranging from six to twenty-five cents were imposed for such transgressions as interrupting calls, leaving the room, using "indecorous" language, or missing a session without a valid excuse.

Three years after its formation the Board had thirty-eight brokers on its roster of members and its initiation fee was set at forty dollars. In contrast to the buttonwood era, meetings were formalized sessions, although there were still no full-time stockbrokers among the membership. The auctions were held in a small room on the second floor of the Bank of the Manhattan Company Building at 40 Wall Street, at brokers' offices, and at other sites. When, however, the Merchants' Exchange Building was constructed in 1827, the Board moved to this location on the square block surrounded by Wall Street, William Street, Hanover Street, and Exchange Place.

In the year of the move to the Merchants' Exchange Building, the Board's listed corporations included—in addition to its various government securities—nineteen insurance companies, twelve banks, the Delaware and Hudson Canal, and the New York Gas Light Company (the country's first public utility). A railroad, the Mohawk and Hudson, was added in 1830. When the Board sought additional data from the concerns on its list to better inform the public about internal changes at these companies, its requests were generally refused without any apologies. Full disclosure, two of today's most widely used buzz words on Wall Street, was not a factor to consider in that period, and many investors bought and sold stock on the basis of rumor alone.

During the 1830s there was more stock trading on the over-the-counter market on the Street than at the indoor auctions run by the New York Stock and Exchange Board, where trading sometimes came to fewer than one hundred shares a day. In fact, the dullest trading day in the history of the Big Board came on March 16, 1830, when only thirty-one shares, worth less than $3,500, changed hands. Initial underwritings were then, as now, a significant part of the entire stock trading mechanism, and yet they were not, then, as now, a function of the Exchange. What's more, the Board did not even have a permanent home between 1835—when 650 financial district buildings, including the Merchants' Exchange, were destroyed by fire—and 1842—when a new Merchants' Exchange Building was completed.

Jacob Little, the first of the long line of great speculators who would make their mark on the floor of the Exchange, put in his appearance at the Board around that time. Unlike previous operators in securities who were more in the foreign mold or part-timers on Wall Street, Little spent all of his time dealing in stocks, as well as planning and executing coups and raids that had the financial community gasping in admiration at his ability.

After starting his career as a clerk, Little founded his own brokerage business in 1835 at the height of an early market boom. Although he was unpopular in the Wall Street community and was even blackballed a number of times before being accepted as a member of the Board, he prospered when others failed in the bear market that followed the panic of 1837. For the next two decades, despite a series of bankruptcies, Little was known as the King of Wall Street because of his skill in short selling and controlling the floating supply of stock in widely traded issues.

For example, one coup in which he participated involved the Morris Canal and Banking Company, whereby Little and others cornered the stock and forced short sellers to meet their demands by keeping their securities off the market. Within a one-month period they pushed the price of Morris Canal from $10 a share to $185 a share before allowing the short sellers to purchase stock to cover their obligations. Similar situations followed over the years until 1856, when Little went broke for the last time, winding up with liabilities of some $10 million. He remained on Wall Street, though, buying and selling odd lots until his death, and according to legend his last words were "I am going up. Who will go with me?"

While Little and other speculators of that period were plying their trade in the auction room of the New York Stock and Exchange Board, there were still many curb-stone brokers—the forerunners of today's American Stock Exchange—who bought and sold stock outdoors. In 1836 a group of these brokers established their own trading auction, called the New Board, to compete with the New York Stock and Exchange Board. But the New Board could not continue to function against the superior markets at the larger organization and was out of business by 1848.

The New Board was neither the first nor the last attempt by others to set up exchanges in New York to deal in some or all of the issues that were traded on the floor of the New York Stock Exchange or its forerunners. These efforts were all unsuccessful, largely because brokerage firms trading on these secondary exchanges were smaller and less financially sound than their competitors at the Big Board. The New York Stock and Exchange Board, furthermore, would not allow its members to trade with those on other exchanges, as witness this resolution passed in 1843:

Resolved that upon the election of any person as a member of the board, who may belong to any other association for the transaction of stock and exchange business, that the person so elected be required to resign such membership before he signs the constitution or takes his seat.

A decade later, with heavy trading volume and a generally static stock market, the Board moved again to the first of several temporary quarters. But as European investors began to sell American securities and banks started to call their loans, a crash hit the market with enormous impact. In 1854 the revelation that executives of the New York and New Haven Railroad had issued fraudulent stock brought about a selling wave, as did other similar scandals that year. Although the Board was conducting two auctions a day, one in the morning and one in the afternoon, it reverted to an honorary presidency around the time of the panic of 1857, rather than have it remain as a salaried position. More than 50 percent of the brokerage firms on the Board went out of business, despite the fact that this panic was far less severe than the one in 1837.

Younger men then tried to purchase membership, but the Board resisted their efforts, terming them unworthy and interlopers. The initiation fee, which was $400 in 1848, was raised to $1,000 nine years later. But the new breed of brokers—who were ruthless and not subject to the amenities of gentlemanly dealings—persisted. By the start of the Civil War they made their weight felt to such an extent that the entire flavor of the floor and the American brokerage business changed in a way that marked a major turning point for both Wall Street and the nation at large.

3

FROM
THE CIVIL WAR
TO THE TWENTIETH
CENTURY

The firing on Fort Sumter on April 12, 1860, marked not only what is considered to be the beginning of the Civil War, but also the start of another depressed period on Wall Street. New York brokers took a loss on the money owed to them by their southern customers, while many banking institutions also felt the break in the national fabric when they fell into bankruptcy. It took about two years before the stock market picked up again, following a string of Union military victories over the Confederacy.

During this wartime period, brokers began to concentrate on a group of stocks in a particular industry, rather than on the entire list. Realizing that no individual could know everything about every stock, members of the Board started to specialize in railroad issues, mining stocks, foreign securities, or another area of concentration. Their customers were still the major institutions or a tiny minority of the population—the limited number of substantial citizens who had the means to make investments—and much of their trading was still for their own private accounts.

In 1863 the New York Stock and Exchange Board changed its name to the now-familiar New York Stock Exchange and a program of reorganization and modernization got under way. There was no doubt that the Exchange was already the most prestigious of the stock exchanges, and within a few years it took over two other entities—the Open Board of Stock Brokers and an organization called the Government Bond Department—to cement its position at the top of the Wall Street scene.

By 1867 battery-powered New York Stock Exchange stock tickers were installed in brokerage firm offices, thereby providing quick information about price changes and eliminating the need for messengers to run back and forth from these offices to the floor. And two years later, stringent financial, accounting, and reporting rules were imposed on listed companies to ensure that brokers and the public obtained more accurate data about their investments.

It was at this time too that foreign investors, particularly those from Great Britain, started to make their weight felt on Wall Street. Foreigners were particularly interested in railroad stocks and bonds and purchased hundreds of millions of dollars' worth of securities in this growing industry as they anticipated its vast development in the years ahead. For members of the Exchange, foreign investment proved to be a boon, since it opened a source of commission business that had been untapped until then. Postwar prosperity in the American industrial world brought with it prosperity in the financial world that was reflected in the rising membership of the Exchange and the increasing revenues that brokers obtained from their expanding activities.

During the 1860s the key figure at the Exchange—and on Wall Street in general—was the financier Jay Cooke. Cooke and his firm floated many hundreds of millions of dollars in government bonds, including a then massive single underwriting of a $500 million issue, through a national syndicate of brokerage firms when the Union was desperately in need of such finances. The success of this underwriting of 6 percent government bonds showed the rest of the financial community the value of reaching out into the heartland of America with a vast sales force and a gigantic publicity blitz for selling stocks and bonds, rather than relying on a small coterie of friends and clients. And it underscored the impact of government securities on the whole securities market, an impact that has increasd significantly in the last century.

With a series of such successes selling government bonds in the United States and Europe, Cooke's firm prospered throughout the decade and became the best known on the Street. But when a financial panic developed in the 1870s and ended the first major mobilization of American investors, Jay Cooke & Co., the leading firm in the financial district, collapsed because it was overextended. The immediate cause was its inability to sell new bonds issued by the Northern Pacific Railroad, which it controlled. The failure of the Cooke firm led to similar bankruptcies among other Exchange members, and the Exchange itself was forced to close for more than a week —marking the first such suspension of trading for more than a day in the Big Board's history. Later actions by President Grant and Secretary of the Treasury William Richardson helped to restore confidence, and the Exchange reopened to operate just as it had before. Cooke lived to see the early years of the twentieth century, but he never regained a fraction of the prestige and power that he wielded during the Civil War and immediately thereafter.

Until 1871 the call auction market was the process by

which stocks were bought and sold on the Exchange. With just two calls a day for buying and selling stocks—at 10:30 A.M. and 1 P.M.—there were only two opportunities to trade in any individual issue. Although some two hundred brokers would attend every day and listen to the request for bids on the entire stock list each morning and afternoon, the opportunities for trading in listed stocks were obviously limited. As a result, periodic moves were made to change this system in favor of one in which more trading in individual stocks could be accomplished.

This change took place in 1871, when a continuous auction market for buying and selling shares at any time during the business day was established. When this move was coupled with the introduction a few years earlier of the tickers that tapped out current prices of securities soon after a trade occurred, the Exchange was always in session, with a two-way auction from 10 A.M. to 3 P.M. on weekdays and from 10 A.M. to noon on Saturdays. Within a few more years brokers obtained telephones—and, with them, immediate access to many sources of information—and thus could place their buy and sell orders as easily off the floor as on. What's more, their customers could just as easily call them to order trades and receive quotations.

In 1873 another of Wall Street's periodic panics brought the nation's economy to a halt and caused the closing of a number of key banks. This panic was a reaction to a similar situation in Europe, which affected the American stock market so much at that time that selling pressure in London, Vienna, Paris, or Berlin was quickly reflected in the United States. Added to the European problems was the monetary crisis caused by the demonetization of silver that took place in the United States the same year. Questions arose about the confidence in the dollar, and gold began to be hoarded by the public.

It was during this era that the specialist system—whereby a man or a group of men acts as brokers' brokers on the Exchange floor by specializing in certain securities and trading in them for their own accounts as well as for those of their customers—developed.

The system started as a fluke in 1875 when a broker named James Boyd broke his leg and was forced to handle all of his business at one spot on the trading floor. Since he did not have the mobility of the other brokers and was confined to one location, he decided to limit his trading to a single stock: the Western Union Company, one of the most popular issues of the day.

Within a few weeks Boyd found that this specialization resulted in more business for him, not only from the public, but also from other brokers who left orders with him at prices that were above or below the current market price. This was the birth of the limit order, a now-popular method of trading whereby the order is not executed until the market price rises or falls to the level at which the order is left with the specialist. As other brokers saw Boyd's business growth, some began specializing in other stocks and the floor soon became a place where brokers representing the public did not buy or sell the stock themselves, but instead took these orders to specialists for execution.

Another of the daring speculators during this time was a powerful, intelligent financial operator with a great sense of self-worth, Jay Gould. Gould, a partner in the firm of Smith, Gould, Martin & Co., was involved in many transactions on and off the floor of the Exchange that ranged from the shady to the outright dishonest.

Perhaps his most outrageous scheme was his tenuous involvement in 1869 of President Ulysses S. Grant in a gold-purchasing scheme that caused losses to investors of millions of dollars. Gould accomplished this contrivance through Abel Corbin, the brother-in-law of the President and a former speculator himself, who introduced Gould to Grant and who appointed a man to a key post in the Treasury Department at Gould's behest.

The way Gould operated here was to purchase gold heavily in the hope—actually a reasonable expectation in view of his shenanigans—that the government would cease its public sales of the metal and thereby cause the price to rise. To ensure government cooperation, Gould also bought some gold for Corbin without requiring any payment until the commodity was sold. The price, of course, continued higher during the period when government sales were discontinued, until Gould learned that the President was about to order the resumption of public gold sales. With Corbin's connivance, this information was kept quiet until Gould had dumped his gold at high prices of up to $160 an ounce. Then, although the dam burst when the government announcement was made and the price plummeted, on September 24, 1869, "Black Friday," Gould made more than $5 million and was neither accused nor convicted of any crime.

In later years, Gould outlived this segment of his life and gained respectability on Wall Street for his work in putting companies—particularly railroads—together into strong financial organizations. His direct or indirect control of two major New York City newspapers, the *Tribune* and the *World*, helped him develop this image as a friend of the people. Even during the panic of 1884 Gould managed to hold his head high and continue his solvency, if not outrageous affluence, when twenty-eight other brokerage firms were forced into bankruptcy. Gould died in 1892, no longer a speculator but a pillar of the Wall Street community that he had once enraged, overwhelmed, and plundered.

In the last decade of the nineteenth century, as the New York Stock Exchange reached its one hundredth anniversary, operational and technological developments brought a new maturity to the organization. A centralized clearinghouse, modeled after the system used by banks, was created for the most active and highest-quality stocks; it enabled brokerage firms to debit and credit their orders with each other without passing stock certificates after every trade. An electric annunciator board was installed to page members without shouting across the room. All listed companies were required to file annual reports, and earnings and balance sheets became a prerequisite for listing. The Exchange at the end of the nineteenth century had 521 member organizations, more than it had in the mid-1970s.

Although the Exchange was primarily seen by its members in those years as a place for trading securities that had already been issued, it was also the home of a new breed of men whose influence was steadily rising on Wall Street. These were the investment bankers, men who would raise the capital needed to launch new companies and create new enterprises. The rise of the investment bankers corresponded with the day of the industrial barons, and the two groups together helped to develop the mass-production economy that has been responsible for much of America's wealth and influence ever since.

Many of the best-known member firms on the New York Stock Exchange today were founded in the years

when investment banking first took hold. These firms all
employed large staffs once they became established and
soon were among the most important in the financial
community. Kuhn Loeb & Co. became one of the first un-
derwriters of industrial companies and owned the controlling interest in some of them before very long. Lehman
Brothers (now Lehman Brothers Kuhn Loeb) and Goldman, Sachs & Co. started in other businesses but became
famous as sellers of various types of securities. Fahne-
stock & Co.; Kidder, Peabody & Co.; and J. & W. Seligman
& Co. also had their birth in this turbulent period late in
the nineteenth century.

But without a doubt the most important name at the
Exchange, and indeed on all of Wall Street, in the nineteenth century was that of a broker and investment
banker named John Pierpont Morgan. J. P. Morgan, who
began as a salesman to financial institutions and then ex-
panded into corporate finance, government securities
sales, and all forms of brokerage and investment banking,
effectively gained control of the New York Central Railroad in 1879, when he was forty-two years old. For many
years thereafter, there was virtually no stopping him.

Prices of stock would rise and fall solely on the basis of
Morgan's decision to stand for a company's board of directors. A spiritual offspring of Jay Gould, Morgan at one
time let President Grover Cleveland know in no uncertain
terms that the credit of the House of Morgan was better
than that of the federal government; in fact, when Morgan paid for a private bond issue in gold, the United
States gold reserves were saved from being decimated.
J. P. Morgan & Co. and its lonely, solitary head were loved
by few but respected by all for their power to move the
world of finance.

Morgan was responsible for the formation at the turn of the century of the United States Steel Corporation—the nation's first billion-dollar enterprise—from a group of independent companies owned by Andrew Carnegie, John D. Rockefeller, and others. He built railroad empires and engaged in multi-million-dollar battles with E. H. Harriman and Jacob Schiff to do so. His advice to a young man inquiring about the course of the stock market—"It will fluctuate"—became legendary. And no name from Wall Street ever passed into the public consciousness as strongly as that of J. P. Morgan.

Although Morgan lived until 1913, he did not have the power on Wall Street in the last years of his life that he did earlier in his career. Some of his interlocking stock holdings were split by the antitrust movement that gained credence under the presidency of Theodore Roosevelt. His efforts to link the New England railroads failed, and his lack of perception about the growing industries of the twentieth century caused him to lose out on many moneymaking opportunities. When he died in Rome, after turning to his companion to say "I've got to go up the hill," he was no longer the titan of the Street who dominated all of the financial markets. But his House —now divided into Morgan Stanley & Co. for the securities business and J. P. Morgan & Co. for commercial banking—continued as the symbol of capitalism and the capital markets in America.

For the Exchange the nineteenth century in effect came to an end in 1903, when it opened its present building at the corner of Broad and Wall streets, constructed at a cost of more than $3 million and with initial annual operating costs of $200,000. The Exchange thus entered the twentieth century in a structure with a huge trading floor topped by a high golden roof. Its solid exterior and its geographical location at the heart of Wall Street identified its position in the center of financial trading in America. The coffee house had now become a palace of finance, and the Exchange was well on its way to become the world's preeminent arena for trading securities.

4

UNTIL ARMAGEDDON

The twentieth century started with the New York Stock Exchange in the midst of a bull market and its members on the floor enjoying a period of financial stability. But those were the days when a bull market was usually followed in a few years by a bear market; stability was followed by panic, which within a few years was followed again by stability. No trend seemed to have any long-lasting endurance, and even the most successful members were constantly on a short rope because of the recognized impermanence of their wealth.

In 1903, for example, a panic hit Wall Street and heavy selling occurred until the end of the summer. The man known as Bet-a-Million Gates, one of the powers in the financial district in that era, said, "I do not believe there was ever a better time to invest in reasonable securities," but no one believed him and the market continued downward. Then the panic—also known as the Rich Man's Panic—suddenly ended as quickly as it began and stock prices turned upward. The professionals on the street turned to other professionals for trading partners, and the market did not again attract the general public in large numbers for another two decades or so.

This emphasis on professional trading in the early

1900s, however, led to the control of all or parts of major companies by the nation's big commercial banks. Although the banks themselves could not own the stock, they formed investment affiliates to do so, resulting in a vast pool of money acting as a speculative force on the market. Insurance companies, in partnership with trust companies and banks, also became heavily involved in securities speculation; and before long, scandals based on collusion and improper dealings erupted. Newspapers railed against the evils of Wall Street, and by 1909 New York Governor Charles Evans Hughes was stirred enough to form a commission to investigate the securities business.

This investigation led to many reforms on the New York Stock Exchange that have continued to this day. Its unlisted securities department—where companies that had no desire to have their shares listed on the Exchange were listed anyway—was abolished. Certain manipulative practices were ruled out, self-regulation was encouraged, and members were prohibited from dealing with bucket shops, shoddy nonmember outfits that were more swindlers than brokers.

Other changes recommended by the commission were the development of rules by the Big Board compelling listed companies to file frequent financial statements and to make them available to the public. But the commission did not come down hard against speculation as a market tool and did not accuse the New York Stock Exchange of any major wrongdoing. In fact, the Exchange as an institution emerged from the investigation in a stronger position than when the commission started its work.

Shortly after World War I began with the assassination of Archduke Francis Ferdinand of Austria-Hungary at

Sarajevo on June 28, 1914, panic selling returned again to Wall Street—but this time in a different format. For it started first in the other financial centers of the world, such as Europe, Canada, and South America, and came to the United States when the decline had already spread widely at these other exchanges. It was not until the end of the war that America replaced London as the financial center of the world and became the place where both bull and bear markets were to originate.

The 1914 panic here was the result of a sharp outflow of gold from this country to Europe to finance the war machines there. Within a three-day period in July, almost every security on the Big Board declined, some by as many as fifteen points. Wall Streeters watched with amazement as trading was suspended on the major exchanges of the world—Vienna, Brussels, Berlin, Rome, Montreal, Madrid, and even St. Petersburg. When the London Stock Exchange closed its doors on July 31 for the first time in its history, the New York exchange was inundated with sell orders from Europe. It had no alternative but to close that day too, before it and the entire securities market would be swamped.

Although the Exchange was closed for only four months in 1914, it was faced with a crisis of major proportions because the outside brokers on New Street, who had long traded securities there in an early version of the over-the-counter market, began buying and selling the stocks listed on the Big Board. To the members of the Exchange who attempted to stop the outdoor trading in their stocks, these brokers were outlaws who were undermining the auction system that had been carefully built up over the years. Yet the outside brokers continued to function during the hiatus of the indoor marketplace, and many New York exchange stocks fell below their July 30 closing prices in over-the-counter trading.

The leaders of the Big Board considered many ways to get the Exchange back into business, ranging from a "Buy a Share of Stock" appeal based on patriotism to a pool of brokerage firms that would purchase stock at an established price to stimulate investor confidence. But cooler heads prevailed and the decision was made to wait until the panic surge receded. In mid-November a clearinghouse established by the Exchange was allowed to begin selling some of its stocks, and an upward price trend quickly became apparent. A month later, trading was resumed on the Exchange—and although there were certain limitations placed on brokers' activities until the following November, the Exchange was effectively back in business again.

During most of the period of World War I, the New York exchange seemed poised for another major bull market. Earnings of the giant corporations spurted and production of industrial goods achieved record levels. Prices of such leading stocks as General Motors, General Electric, and U. S. Steel soared to new highs and brokers enjoyed times of prosperity all through the era of formal United States neutrality and the days of the country's entry into the war.

In fact, a new generation of stockholders was created for the members of the Big Board in 1917 and 1918 when the purchase of government bonds and stock in companies that made armaments for the war effort was for many people the patriotic thing to do. A large number of these purchases were made in odd lots—quantities of fewer than one hundred shares—as the investors involved could not afford to buy any more. Later some of these investors became affluent and thereby better and more frequent customers for the brokerage fraternity on the floor.

After the war ended, however, the market dropped steadily for a few years and the atmosphere on Wall Street again became glum. In an early example of "jawboning," President Warren Harding called in businessmen and financial leaders to demand actions that would turn the tide, but the decline continued anyhow. Business inventories fell sharply, and there seemed to be another panic on the way.

A full-scale panic did not, however, recur on Wall Street, as the economy righted itself in the early 1920s. The stock market felt the impact of a sharp increase in capital spending, the development of new technology, and the growth of American investment overseas—and it reacted accordingly. Optimism prevailed on the floor, and by 1924 the euphoria was flying so high that common stock prices began what was then their most concerted powerful upward movement in history.

A look at some of the statistics demonstrates the strength of the huge bull market that occurred between 1924 and 1929. In 1924 there were some 433 million listed shares on the Big Board with a market value of $27 billion. Five years later the number of shares had risen to more than one billion, while the market value had more than tripled, to almost $90 billion.

This was also the time when syndicates became the predominant method of handling underwritings of new common stock by brokers and investment bankers. An underwriting of $20 million, $30 million, or more was too much for a single member of the Exchange to handle— and so firms banded together in a formalized manner both to raise the capital and to share the risk. Every syndicate was temporary, moreover, remaining in effect only while the underwriting was under way and breaking up when the securities were all sold or could no longer be sold. One firm usually led the syndicate as its manager and others came in as members, not only for the profit potential but also because of the realization that they might soon manage a syndicate and expect the other firms to join it.

Hundreds of thousands of men and women—women had few management positions then—were working in the nation's financial markets, although they represented a small fraction of those in the agricultural and mining fields. Yet the salaries of those in the financial community equaled the amounts paid to those in agriculture and mining combined. Wall Street was a lucrative area for employment in the twenties, and members of the New York Stock Exchange were in the most lucrative spot of all.

Among the members of this Wall Street establishment were some manipulators who managed successfully to stay within the bounds of the law as it then existed, regardless of the morality of their activities. One of the most effective during the roaring twenties was Jesse Livermore, a former bucket-shop operator who was known as the King of the Speculators. Livermore did not try to control the entire market, but just those stocks in which he wanted to take a position. Having said, "I never go into a trade unless I see at least ten points profit," he achieved his goal more often than not.

One of Livermore's most effective manipulations was his bull pool whereby a group he led conspired to push the market price higher in the stock of Piggly-Wiggly Stores. This was done in order to help Clarence Saunders, president of the regional supermarket chain, sell new stock at a higher price. Livermore managed to corner the floating supply of Piggly-Wiggly stock, a move that tripled the price within a thirty-day period. Livermore left the pool when he realized that Saunders had other intentions in addition to floating new stock, but he had already accomplished a coup that is talked about on the floor to this day.

Another of the great speculators of that time was Michael J. Meehan, an Irishman who was born in England and emigrated to the United States, working initially as a messenger and then as a ticket broker. After first establishing himself uptown, he moved his office to 20 Broad Street in downtown New York, where he came to know many brokers and learned that there was more money to be made in securities than in theater tickets. As a result, he bought a seat on the Curb Exchange (now the American Stock Exchange) and in 1920 moved over to the New York Stock Exchange, where he was to become one of its most prominent brokers. His firm, M. J. Meehan & Co., eventually held eight memberships on the Big Board, more than any other commission brokerage firm at the time.

Meehan was a red-headed, bare-knuckle fighter and brought his flair for the spectacular and dramatic to the floor of the Exchange at a period when these characteristics were extremely useful for success. Meehan was frequently in the middle of a number of bull manipulations in the violent trading of the 1920s—such as the one that pushed the company now called RCA Corporation up more than sixty points in four days. A born salesman, he could convince men and women in all income brackets of the merits of buying and selling certain stocks when few others could get the public to respond. He even opened offices on transatlantic luxury liners to develop business from the passengers who could not stay away from the market.

Meehan was also one of the few to anticipate that the heated economy of the 1920s was leading to trouble, even though he participated in the overheating process. In his later years he bought control of the Good Humor Corp. and spent much of his time there when Wall Street was a disaster area. He sold much of his stock before the crash and thereby was able to recover when many of his contemporaries were failing. A friend once asked him, "Do you want to be the richest broker in the cemetery?" and Meehan replied puckishly, "It's all on paper—it's all on paper."

Meehan's *bête noire* was Joseph P. Kennedy—the Wall Streeter who was later named the first head of the Securities and Exchange Commission. During the Great Depression the SEC investigated many of the Meehan dealings on the floor, and although it cleared him of criminal charges it expelled him from all securities exchanges for stock manipulation. Afterward, one of Meehan's happiest memories was that he threw Kennedy out of his office when the head of the political dynasty came in to ask for a campaign contribution for the Democratic Party.

Other prominent floor traders of the day included Frank Bliss, Joseph Higgins, and Louis Zimmerman, all of whom could disguise their intentions so carefully that they were able to push up prices in short periods before any of their competitors realized what was taking place. Before 1929 there were few bears to compete with these bulls—many of whom were outside the White Anglo-Saxon Protestant power structure, interested solely in the market rather than the companies whose shares were bought and sold, and often involved in speculation for speculation's sake.

The technique that members of the Exchange and their customers engaged in to excess during those years, and the one that helped lead to the crash of 1929, was buying on margin. Investors would borrow much of the money used to purchase stocks and bonds from their brokers, who would then hold the stock as security for the loan. As long as prices continued to rise, the loans could be repaid with interest and customers and brokers would make a profit. But when prices declined to any major extent, the borrower would owe more than his collateral was worth and would be asked to come up with the difference. And if he could not handle this margin call, the stock would be sold, thereby precipitating still further declines.

Stock market credit amounted to a whopping $8.5 billion in 1929, more than $3 billion greater than it is today in a substantially larger economy. Brokers had principally obtained their money to extend margin loans to customers by borrowing from banks, but with this overheated credit system in operation, corporations also began lending money to brokers. Highly leveraged financial trusts with little common stock in their capitalization but with a substantial amount of debt also became a major element of the investment scene—a situation that led to further pyramiding and to further economic expansion.

Thus the stage was set for the most severe plummeting of stock prices in the history of the Big Board. On October 29, 1929, far more shares were traded there than had ever been traded before and the depression officially began. The New York Stock Exchange would never be the same again.

5

BUILDING
THE BIG BOARD

The Great Depression on Wall Street did not, of course, develop in a vacuum. Many factors contributed to this plunge in stock prices on the floor of the New York Stock Exchange and the accompanying losses in the values of securities held by millions. And one of the most significant was the false optimism about unending prosperity that pervaded the nation.

As surprising as the precipitous decline of 1929 was to most people, there were nevertheless some who anticipated a sharp downturn. Two of the smartest speculators of that era, Joseph P. Kennedy and Bernard Baruch, started selling their stocks in 1928 in anticipation of a fall. A number of investment services warned about the end of the bull market of the 1920s, and a few well-known economists of that period were publicly bearish with predictions that unfavorable changes in business conditions were imminent. Toward the end of 1928 the Federal Reserve Board even raised the discount rate a few times and sold government bonds in an effort to curb speculative excesses, but these restraints failed to stem the tide.

Whatever clouds were on the horizon, the general attitude among brokers was still by and large one of euphoria. For instance, on January 11, 1929, Robert L. Leeds bought a seat on the Exchange for $600,000 and, finding that the turmoil of the floor was not for him, sold it about a month later for $625,000 to return to his family business, the Manhattan Shirt Company. Whether it was an astute analysis of what was in store for the market or just plain luck, Leeds managed to get into and out of the Exchange community at a profit only months before the greatest decline in its history.

By the middle of 1929 prices on European stock markets were off sharply and the building and automotive industries in the United States were suffering from poor business. Manipulations and pools were still carried out on the floor, bringing riches to those involved, but overall economic conditions grew steadily worse, regardless of the cheerful pronouncements made periodically by brokers and government officials to boost the public's morale. Wall Streeters in general saw no panic on the horizon when autumn arrived, and until mid-October there was hardly a trace of concern about the future of stock prices.

Yet the cataclysmic crash nevertheless came on October 29—the famous *Variety* headline read: "Wall Street Lays an Egg"—and plunged the nation into gloom and its deepest economic depression. The situation grew worse in 1930 and 1931, despite the statements to the contrary of President Herbert Hoover, and the stock market did not bottom out until June 1932. During the period from August 1929 to June 1932, the value of securities listed on the Exchange plummeted from about $90 billion to $16 billion and brokers by the hundreds—along with many of their customers—were wiped out. The price of a membership, or seat, on the Exchange similarly dropped from

$625,000 (including a right to buy a one-fourth interest in another seat) in 1929 to $68,000 in 1932.

The year 1932, when the plummet finally ended and stocks were worth about 12 percent of their pre-crash value, brought the election of President Franklin D. Roosevelt and the emergence of the New Deal, with its attendant emphasis on the government's role in overseeing and regulating business. In the years immediately prior to the New Deal, the Exchange made some efforts on its own to root out the manipulative devices that were used on the floor, but these efforts were largely ineffectual. It was left to the Roosevelt administration and the new Congress, therefore, to get to the heart of the disillusion of the public with the unethical, if not dishonest, dealings then occurring on Wall Street.

The major investigation of that era was undertaken by a subcommittee of the Senate Committee on Banking and Currency, whose counsel was Ferdinand Pecora. The Pecora Committee, as the group came to be called, found that brokers' customers were not adequately protected against fraud and deception and that there was a great deal of conduct on the Street inconsistent with just and equitable principles of trade. Examples of many swindles perpetrated upon the public by brokers were laid upon the record, creating a furore that did not subside until new legislation was passed.

One major result of these revelations was the passage of the Securities Act of 1933 and the Securities Exchange Act of 1934—two landmark laws that created the Securities and Exchange Commission, provided for full disclosure to the public, prohibited manipulations, called for registration of new securities issues, and firmly established the concept of self-regulation by securities exchanges.

Another important piece of legislation of that era affecting the securities business was the Banking Act of 1933, commonly called the Glass-Steagall Act. Among its provisions, the law forced commercial banks to dispose of their investment affiliates because of undue concentration of power when both functions were joined under a single ownership and management. The new investment banking concerns, many of which later became brokers as well, included Morgan Stanley & Co., an offshoot of J. P. Morgan & Co., and the First Boston Corporation, an offshoot of the First National Bank of Boston and the Chase National Bank. One commercial bank, however, Brown Brothers Harriman & Co., received special dispensation to continue as a member of the Exchange.

In the following year the Securities and Exchange Commission was established to enforce the two securities laws, with Kennedy, the former speculator, as its first chairman. Kennedy was succeeded by James Landis, who was followed in the post by William O. Douglas, later an Associate Justice of the Supreme Court. By 1940, after Douglas resigned as chairman of the SEC, there was such a myriad of regulatory programs by which the federal government attempted to prevent any return to the pre-1929 patterns on the floor that the Exchange had to recognize the power of Washington before making any formal decisions that would change the nature of its organization and structure.

During this period a new era was also dawning at the Exchange. The Richard Whitney scandal, in which a former president of the Exchange was convicted of grand larceny, led to the appointment of a committee to study the administration of the Big Board, which recommended that a full-time paid president be named. The person elected to that position, in 1938, was William McChesney Martin, Jr., then a young partner of the member firm of A. G. Edwards & Sons in St. Louis and later the longtime chairman of the Federal Reserve Board.

The professional management staff installed under Martin reported to a thirty-three-man board of governors, which represented a reduction of seventeen from the previous unwieldy governing board. The new governors were the president and chief executive officer, twenty-nine representatives of the securities industry, and three people to represent the public interest. The staff of the Exchange was organized by department and division, and the free-wheeling nature of the floor was reined in somewhat by rules and regulations imposed by this staff.

During World War II the floor was a quiet place, with many brokers, specialists, and employees in the armed forces and the economy geared to production for the war effort. The president of the Exchange in those years was Emil Schram, a former chairman of the Reconstruction Finance Corporation, while the two chairmen elected by the Big Board over a four-year period were the veteran specialists Robert Stott and John A. Coleman. Although average daily volume of shares traded on the floor almost doubled between 1940 and 1944 to over 1.4 million shares, it was still less than half of the 1930 average daily volume of more than 2.9 million shares.

During the years immediately after the end of the war, the nation's wartime production was converted back to peacetime uses, as the vast pent-up consumer needs for housing, automobiles, furniture, appliances, and soft goods began to be filled. The sale of new securities of the nation's big corporations, coupled with the ability to buy and sell existing securities of these companies on the floor of the Exchange, would have to be a prime factor in fueling this boom. But there was relatively little public interest in the stock market, and the floor reflected this lack of interest with a noticeable lack of activity. Few stocks sold at a price-earnings ratio—their market price divided by the company's per-share earnings for the year—as high as ten, indicating the unenthusiastic climate of the time.

G. Keith Funston was elected president of the Exchange in 1951 and soon instituted a program to attract more young and less affluent individuals to the investment process. "Own Your Share of American Business" was the Exchange's theme, which, when backed up by the marketing efforts of commission brokerage firms, became a means to lure millions of Americans into the stock market. Even though Saturday trading ended in 1952, the number of individual shareholders rose from almost 6.5 million that year to more than 8.5 million in 1956 and about 12.5 million in 1959. A bull market was under way in full force during the 1950s, as both individuals and financial institutions—such as mutual funds, pension funds, tax-exempt foundations, and trust companies— brought billions of dollars' worth of orders to their brokers on the floor for execution.

The bull market, called the Eisenhower bull market for the then President, brought great wealth to the Exchange specialists in some of the popular and widely traded issues. The best-known names of American industry— including American Telephone & Telegraph, General Electric, General Motors, Texaco, and Union Carbide— were the stocks most heavily in demand, and the posts where trading was done in these issues were unusually busy. Toward the end of the decade, glamour and science-based stocks like Eastman Kodak, Texas Instruments, Polaroid, and Litton Industries equaled, and even surpassed, the old blue chips in public attention, and their specialists, too, were swamped with orders as each new technological development surfaced.

In the early 1960s, under the presidency of John F. Kennedy, the bull market continued to roar. While low-priced stocks (many of which were traded on the American Stock Exchange and the over-the-counter market) were in the forefront, most Big Board issues continued to move forward in price amid strong volume. Although warning after warning against excessive speculation was issued by the Exchange and individual brokerage firms, this frenzy continued until 1962, when the bubble burst.

This was the year that inflation was brought somewhat under control and many investors came to the conclusion that prices could not increase forever. A severe market break in May 1962 was the result, during which the Exchange had its first nine-million-share day since 1933. The SEC's Special Study of Securities Markets in 1963 could not pinpoint any specific reason for the severe decline. But it did emphatically state that "contrary to some speculation at the time that the events might be the result of some conspiracy, [there is no] evidence that the break was deliberately precipitated by any group or resulted from manipulation or illegal conduct in the functioning of the market."

In 1967 Robert W. Haack stepped into the presidency of the Exchange, just about the time that a "back office" crisis hit the Big Board and almost paralyzed the trading process on the floor. A sudden and unexpected upsurge in trading took place and the facilities in brokers' offices to handle this vast amount of paper work proved inadequate. Stock certificates were lost or delayed, purchase and sale confirmations were misrouted, and written communications among brokers became bogged down in the system.

To ease the pressure on member organizations, the Exchange reduced the trading hours on the floor in August 1967 and again in January 1968. During the summer of that year, the Exchange floor was also closed one day a week, so that the time could be used to process the backlog of securities that had not been received or delivered. It wasn't until January 1969 that a five-day operation was restored, and the full trading day on the floor did not resume until May 1970.

Along with the paper-work crunch of the late 1960s came a period of deep financial trouble for many member firms of the Exchange. The number of member firms sank from 647 in 1967 to 572 in 1970 as a result of a wave of bankruptcies, mergers, and acquisitions on Wall Street. Although relatively few customers lost any money or securities held by a broker, the industry was brought to a virtual standstill until the logjam was broken by the introduction of new methodology. Almost concurrently, the healthy brokerage firms agreed to contribute to a fund to compensate the customers of the firms that could not meet their obligations. The Exchange's own program to do this was superseded in 1970 by the Securities Investor Protection Corporation, chartered by Congress to protect customers' cash and securities holdings up to a defined limit in the event of future liquidations.

Following Haack's resignation in 1972, James J. Needham, a former commissioner of the SEC, was named chairman and chief executive officer under a reorganization of the Exchange. During his chairmanship in 1973 the Exchange established the Depository Trust Company to hold stock certificates and transfer them by bookkeeping entry rather than by physical delivery. Five hundred billion dollars' worth of securities involving over 34 million individual transactions were settled through this system in 1978, with DTC holding on deposit at the end of that year 6.9 billion shares, representing more than 13,000 different common and preferred stocks, and debt securities valued at over $25 billion. The Exchange now owns 44.3 percent of DTC.

Other instances of automation of the facilities on the floor in recent years include the Common Message Switch, an interface between the Exchange's communications system and the systems of member firms to transmit orders and reports of transactions; Market Data System II, which captures and displays information from the floor; and the Designated Order Turnaround (DOT) system, which transmits market orders up to 299 shares and limit orders up to 500 shares directly from the member firms to the specialist without going through a floor broker. All odd-lot (fewer than one hundred shares) stock trading and nonconvertible bond trading have been computerized too.

The 1970s also saw the end of the historic fixed brokerage commission rate structure, which had been a standard fixture at the Exchange since its founding. Unfixed commissions—whereby customers could negotiate with their brokers the price they would pay for the purchase and sale of securities and brokers would similarly negotiate with Exchange members on the floor for actual execution—came in stages, prompted by Congress and the SEC. First rates on orders exceeding $500,000 were unfixed in 1971; then commissions on orders over $300,000 became negotiated the following year. Orders of $2,000 or less were added in 1974 and all public trading rates were unfixed on "May Day," May 1, 1975. A similar rule for execution of orders on the floor by members there went into effect exactly one year later.

One of the effects of negotiated commissions has been the development of a two-tier pricing structure whereby large institutional investors are paying substantially lower fees for transacting their orders, while most individual investors are paying about the same as or more than they did before the unfixing of rates. Brokers have been offering institutions discounts of up to 85 percent off the old fixed rates, bringing some prices down to eight or ten cents a share, while prices charged to individuals—including those who buy from discount brokers and who purchase large amounts of securities—are down only an average of about 8 percent. Since institutions account for around 60 percent of all public trading on the Big Board, the revenue to brokers on the floor and off has therefore been cut significantly by negotiated commissions.

In May 1976 Needham was forced out of the chairmanship of the Exchange and William M. Batten, a retired chairman of the J. C. Penney Company, succeeded him in the post. Batten, who was nurtured on fierce competition, has accepted the unfixed rate structure and is directing the Exchange as it attempts to move into new categories of trading, such as financial futures and options.

The New York Stock Exchange that is nearing its two hundredth anniversary is therefore a vastly different institution from the small organization that was formed at Corre's Hotel. It now has more than a thousand members and provides the primary site for trading the securities of the majority of the nation's largest, most widely held corporations. Close to 30 billion shares are listed on the Big Board, with a market value of over $900 billion. Whatever the shape of the national market system that emerges under pressure from Washington in the 1980s, the New York Stock Exchange is likely to be an active and dominant participant—and to continue as a major force in the growth and development of the nation's economy.

PART III

The Top Men

6   RICHARD WHITNEY:
A BLUE BLOOD
GOES BAD

Although the floor of the New York Stock Exchange has seen its share of scoundrels and scandals over the years, no one has been as famous in his infamy there as Richard Whitney. A blue blood, a president of the Big Board, a rajah among Brahmins, a personification of the White Anglo-Saxon Protestant Eastern Seaboard Establishment, Whitney was the highest and mightiest of all the members of the Exchange to fall from grace into disgrace.

What brought Whitney down, oddly enough, was poor investments that a sophisticated stockbroker should never have allowed himself to get into. There were some obscure Florida firms and a liquor company that did not prosper after Repeal into which he poured enormous amounts of borrowed money as the prices moved steadily downward. Since he had borrowed funds to pay for these stocks, he had to find the money for repayment when the loans came due, and eventually embezzled it from others. As a result he was sent to jail in 1938 and lost not only his liberty but also the prestige that had placed him among Wall Street's finest.

This prestige reached its pinnacle during the worst moments of the Exchange, the Great Crash of 1929, when Whitney attempted with great courage and faith in the market system to stem the decline. Although he failed to single-handedly halt the plunge, he came to symbolize the struggle of Wall Street to work itself out of the depression and was elected the youngest president of the Big Board in 1930. He held that post before salaried chief executives were hired, and served with distinction as the chief spokesman and lobbyist for the Exchange for five one-year terms before word of his financial difficulties leaked out to the Exchange or the public.

The scandal that proved to be Whitney's downfall was unexpected by the many who saw him as an example of perfect probity. His family had been in the country since his Pilgrim ancestor John Winthrop arrived in 1630 on the *Arbella.* Some of his ancestors had been merchants in the India trade, and the Whitneys were one of the New England families that prospered with the development of America. Richard Whitney's father was president of a small Boston bank, and his uncle Edward was a correspondent banker there for J. P. Morgan & Co.

Richard Whitney was born in 1888 in Beverly, Massachusetts, a suburb of Boston, and followed the conventional path of a scion of an old and wealthy Bay State family. He went to Groton, where he was a good student, captain of the baseball team, and treasurer of the summer camp. His next stop was Harvard, where he made the varsity crew, was named to the rich and fashionable Porcellian Club, and graduated in 1910 by completing the required courses in just three years.

Whitney's first job in the securities business was with Kidder, Peabody & Co. at its Boston office, where he spent a year. But by then Edward Whitney, who had married the daughter of a Morgan partner, was a partner of J. P. Morgan in New York. Richard's brother George had been working for the same firm for a couple of years. As a result, Dick Whitney also wanted to come to New York and participate in the larger financial scene. "There was not enough happening in Boston" was the way he put it when he left.

After arriving in New York, Whitney joined the brokerage firm of Potter, Choate & Prentice, where he made very rapid progress. Of course, his close contacts at the House of Morgan did not hurt his career development and he was able to obtain a number of large orders for his firm. In 1912, before reaching his twenty-fourth birthday, he bought a seat on the Big Board and two years later became a partner of the old-line brokerage house of Cumings & Marckwald.

By 1916—shortly after he married Mrs. Gertrude Sheldon Sands, an attractive young widow whose father was a president of the Union League Club—the name of this firm was changed to Richard Whitney & Co. He climbed quickly into the inner circle on the floor, became known throughout the worlds of business and finance, and, although he spent two years in Washington during World War I as a dollar-a-year man for the Food Administration, was elected a member of the Big Board's governing board (as its policy-making body was then called) in 1919.

Through the long years of President Coolidge's bull market, Whitney served as one of the principal brokerage agents for J. P. Morgan. Although his profile bulged a bit below the chest, Whitney was always impeccably dressed. A big man physically, standing six feet tall and weighing 210 pounds, he carried his body proudly, with the agility of an athlete. His features were large, his brow was square, his shoulders were broad, and his eyes were deep-set under prominent, downward-slanting eyebrows.

He was the very picture of a successful floor broker with wealth, breeding, and experience.

Off the floor, Whitney enjoyed the good life, with a $100,000 town house in Manhattan and a 231-acre estate in the fox-hunting country of Far Hills, New Jersey. In addition to riding to hounds, he played tennis, owned a stable of thoroughbred horses, was elected treasurer of the New York Yacht Club, and belonged to all of the other "right" clubs in town—the Links, the Turf & Field, the Racquet, and the Knickerbocker. His maintenance bills alone ran to more than $5,000 a month. Dick Whitney had arrived.

Nevertheless, Whitney was thrust further into the limelight entirely by accident. In 1928 he was elected a vicepresident of the Exchange and expected to spend a number of years there in relative obscurity. But when the unexpected debacle of the crash arrived on Wall Street in October 1929, the veteran president of the Big Board, E. H. H. Simmons, was in Hawaii on his honeymoon. J. P. Morgan himself was in England. As the senior officer present, Whitney was in charge and was galvanized into action.

Through most of October the market threatened to explode downward, and by Thursday, October 24, conditions were grim. Almost 13 million shares changed hands as investors panicked and prices plunged into an abyss. With fear ruling the market, Whitney realized that some drastic steps were necessary. So at 1:30 P.M., after an emergency meeting at the J. P. Morgan offices, the tall, thick-shouldered, elegantly suited Whitney, his Porcellian pig dangling from a watch chain stretched across his generous paunch, strolled across the floor to Post 2, where U. S. Steel was traded, and roared, "I bid 205 for 10,000

Steel." Those words became the most famous single order in stock market history.

The grandness of this gesture was not so much the large purchase order placed at a time when only sellers were on the floor but the price of the order. For 205 was well above the offering price, then under 200, and Whitney was thus telling jittery brokers and investors that he—and indirectly the J. P. Morgan bank and its allies—had enough confidence in the economy to bid for this bell-wether security on the Exchange at a higher price than required, with the apparent foreknowledge that such an investment would prove profitable. In fact, Whitney purchased only 200 of the 10,000 shares he had offered to buy, but the symbolism of the episode caught the eye of thousands of panicky speculators. Whitney also marched up to other posts and placed additional orders for blue-chip securities with an aggregate value of $20 million. The newspaper headlines on October 25 told of the effect of Whitney's flamboyant moves: "Richard Whitney Halts Stock Panic . . . Worst Stock Crash Stemmed by Banks . . . Heroic Action Rallies Market." Although prices closed lower on October 24, they were substantially higher than their lows of the day.

Unfortunately the halt in the market proved to be short-lived and October 29 became "Black Tuesday," the darkest day in the Exchange's history, when 16,410,000 shares were traded—less than one quarter of the record 81,600,000 shares traded on October 10, 1979, but nevertheless a tremendous amount for that era and the equivalent of well over 400 million shares today. The Dow Jones Industrial Average fell by more than thirty points, marking a one-day decline of 11.7 percent and a loss of $6.7 billion in investors' portfolios. The losses in major issues were immense, including twenty-eight-point declines in such giants of the economy as American Telephone & Telegraph and General Electric. Some stocks could hardly be given away.

Whitney called a meeting that day of the governing board in a tiny room in the basement to discuss whether to close the Exchange, as during the panic of 1873 and at the beginning of World War I. Because Whitney termed it unthinkable to close and was able to influence the others to think likewise, the Exchange remained open on Wednesday and on Thursday morning, after which it was closed until the following Monday to give the harried staff a chance to catch up with the overflow of paper work. Whitney made this announcement to the members of the Exchange while the stock tickers clattered behind him, in an attempt to convince the public that all problems were well in hand.

For the next few weeks, Whitney—who was also the chairman of the Exchange's business conduct committee—went around the floor, to public meetings, and to private conferences exuding all the charm and confidence he possessed in an effort to bolster the attitudes of his comrades. Once, after a governing board meeting at J. P. Morgan's 23 Wall Street headquarters, Whitney was overheard telling his associates as they left the room to cross Broad Street to the Exchange, "Now get your smiles on, boys." Whitney was an island of tranquillity amid the storm. His leadership ability helped to steady the sagging morale of his fellow brokers until a turn in the market developed in mid-November that marked the end of the first phase of Wall Street's own particular depression.

On November 30 the governors of the Exchange passed a resolution expressing appreciation of Whitney's contribution during the days of crisis, noting that "great emergencies produce the men who are competent to deal with them. . . . Leadership devolved upon Mr. Richard Whitney, vice president of the Exchange, who exhibited the required qualifications to such a high degree that the storm was successfully weathered and the prestige of the Exchange maintained and strengthened." The press reported his public appearances as it would those of a popular entertainer. "Richard Whitney, acting president of the Exchange, hat tilted on his head at a jaunty angle, sauntered nonchalantly across the floor half an hour before closing time and left the room with a debonair smile," enthused one reporter.

In 1930, at the age of forty-one, Whitney was elected to the first of his five terms as president of the Big Board and had reached the pinnacle of influence and power on Wall Street. He wrote effusively about competition and free enterprise, testified before congressional committees about capitalism and the New York Stock Exchange, met with President Herbert Hoover as the leading representative of the financial community, and even received for his office lobby the Post 2 where he had made his famous bid for U. S. Steel when that post was replaced by another type of construction. He was called by many "The Voice of Wall Street." Some considered him highhanded, but few questioned his ability as the head of the Exchange. Furthermore, according to documents made public by the Senate Committee on Banking and Currency, Whitney's public service was not injurious to the income of his firm. Its profits were $313,000 in 1928, $1,112,000 in 1929, $516,000 in 1930, $231,000 in 1931, $171,000 in 1932, and $231,000 in 1933.

Despite these eloquent figures, Whitney's own personal

finances were never as strong as they seemed. Always in the shadow of his older brother, George, by then a senior partner of J. P. Morgan & Co., Richard Whitney was frequently in the habit of borrowing money to get past temporary emergencies. And when he began putting funds into unsuccessful speculative stocks, his finances started to fall apart, never to recover.

Even before the Great Crash, Whitney had been investing in such unknown companies as the Florida Humus Company and Colloidal Products Corporation of America. Another horrendous investment was the Distilled Liquors Corporation, a producer during Prohibition of the bootleg applejack called Jersey Lightning, which failed to catch on later as he had expected. George Whitney continued to lend him money for these and other disastrous ventures, without telling his partners at J. P. Morgan the full extent of the loans from company funds. By 1931 Dick Whitney was in debt for close to $2 million.

Nevertheless, borrowing in the millions of dollars continued, from banks, from George Whitney, from J. P. Morgan & Co., and from others in the Exchange community. Richard Whitney had many unsecured loans of $100,000 outstanding—often verbal agreements to repay in thirty or ninety days, which were just as often ignored because the funds were not available. He was desperate enough in 1936 to make unauthorized use of $150,000 worth of securities that belonged to the New York Yacht Club, of which he was treasurer, as collateral for a $200,000 loan to his firm.

It was in the following year, however, that Whitney committed the larceny that led to his conviction and jailing. A trustee of the Stock Exchange Gratuity Fund as well as the broker for the fund, Whitney was told by his

fellow trustees in February to sell $350,000 worth of
bonds and buy other securities with the proceeds. Whitney did so, but kept the new bonds instead of placing
them in the custody of the fund. He took similar action
later in 1937, so that by the end of the year he had personally kept some $1 million worth of securities and cash
that should have been held by the fund, and which he
used as debt collateral.

In November 1937, when Whitney was absent from a
meeting of the fund trustees, a clerk summoned the nerve
to inform the group that Whitney had been holding on to
its securities and cash for such an extensive period of
time. The chairman of the trustees contacted Whitney
and told him to deliver the fund's property immediately,
and Whitney—with just $75,000 in his own and his firm's
accounts—had his back against the wall. In desperation,
he blurted out the truth to his brother George. "I asked
him how he could have done it," George Whitney later
recalled, "and he said he had no explanation to
offer."

George came through again by providing more than
$1 million to allow Richard to repay the fund, even
though the older brother had to withdraw money from
his share of the Morgan partnership to do so. But although Richard Whitney's problems with the fund were
kept private, rumors had spread around the entire floor
that he was in financial difficulty. He had borrowed or
asked to borrow from so many individuals that his lack of
funds to pay his obligations had virtually become general
knowledge on Wall Street.

One result of his situation was that when distress
selling developed in the stock of the Greyhound Corporation in January 1938, the specialist suspected that Whit-

ney's firm was in trouble and relayed his fears to the governors. As it happened, Whitney was not involved in the sale of Greyhound, but because of his previous peccadillos was the one whose name immediately came to mind. A questionnaire about his firm's financial condition was sent to him by the Exchange, and his answers, even with falsifications, showed that its capital position did not meet the standards set by the Big Board.

The Exchange then sent an accountant to study the books and records at the Whitney firm; the accountant reported that there was evidence that customers' securities had been misappropriated. Even though Whitney tried to stall the investigation—and, in a final dishonest attempt to get his firm back into the black, embezzled securities belonging to his customers, including his father-in-law's estate—he finally realized that he could go on no longer. He offered to sell his membership if charges against him were dropped, explaining to the governors, "I mean the Stock Exchange to millions of people."

The governors proceeded, however, and at 9 A.M. on March 7, 1938, the board's business conduct committee met to inquire formally of the Whitney firm whether it could meet its obligations. When the answer was, as it had to be, negative, the bell was rung from the rostrum overlooking the floor prior to the start of trading and an announcement was made to a silent membership that Richard Whitney & Co. was suspended from the Exchange for insolvency. It turned out that Whitney had borrowed more than $25 million in four months and that his firm was $11 million in the red.

Within a few days, Whitney was booked on various charges of misappropriation and defalcation and shortly afterward pleaded guilty to three charges of grand larceny. Called by the judge a "public betrayer," he was sentenced to five to ten years in Sing Sing and began his term in April, as a crowd in the street outside his home watched him depart for jail. Although his brother George, with fraternal fealty, eventually repaid all the money that had been borrowed or stolen, Richard Whitney was gone from Wall Street forever and the Big Board was soon to acquiesce to the Securities and Exchange Commission's demand that a paid, full-time president be elected.

In prison, Whitney was a celebrity from the very first day. On one occasion an official there announced, "All men who came Thursday, Friday, Saturday, Monday, or Tuesday and Mr. Whitney please step out of their cells." Convicts and guards alike deferentially asked for his autograph, and he was selected to welcome new arrivals to the prison by handing out cartons of cigarettes to them. When the New York Stock Exchange baseball team traveled up to Ossining to play the convicts, their eyes were on Whitney sitting in the stands as much as they were on the ball. The warden called him a model prisoner.

Three years and four months later—the earliest possible time for his release on parole—Whitney left Sing Sing, in August 1941, carrying a brown paper parcel in one hand and an onion sack containing his belongings in the other. "I have not a word to say" was his response to reporters who had waited on the prison steps for his release. George Whitney, ever reliable and now president of J. P. Morgan & Co., was there in a limousine as his brother Richard, now fifty-three years old, came out to drive off to a secluded family-owned dairy farm near Barnstable on Cape Cod, Massachusetts, that he was to manage. Richard Whitney, once a millionaire, left prison with $181.01 to his name and lived out the rest of his days until his death in 1974, at the age of eighty-six, far from the power and the glory of Wall Street.

7 WILLIAM McCHESNEY MARTIN, JR.: THE CONSCIENCE OF THE EXCHANGE

On December 8, 1937, the New York Stock Exchange established a committee to investigate "all aspects of a further development of organization and administration of the Exchange [and] study the Exchange's organization and administration with a view to radical reform." It was formally called the Committee for the Study of the Organization and Administration of the New York Stock Exchange, but was known on the street as the Conway Committee because its chairman was Carle Conway, chairman of the Continental Can Company. And from its deliberations came the impetus to restructure the Big Board into a format in which for the first time in about eighty years a paid president would be at the helm.

The man selected for that formidable position was William McChesney Martin, Jr., a thirty-one-year-old, relatively new member of the Exchange who had already earned a reputation as an intellectual and scholar who knew his way around the market. Called the Boy Wonder of Wall Street, Martin headed the Big Board for three years, during which it was coming under increasing attack from the Securities and Exchange Commission. And by the time that he entered the Army in 1941 and turned the reins over to Emil Schram, he had managed, despite the pressures from Washington, to ensure that the New York exchange would retain its independence as a self-regulatory organization.

Martin later went on to bigger and better things as a longtime chairman of the Federal Reserve Board. At the end of his career he returned to the Big Board as a consultant and developed a report that provided for another major internal reorganization. Some called him the greatest American public servant of the twentieth century. But it was his initial service as president of the Exchange during one of its periods of greatest crisis that marked him as a leader in the financial community and a giant in Wall Street history.

When Martin arrived at the New York Stock Exchange headquarters as president on June 30, 1938, the situation was grim. Richard Whitney, an aristocratic pillar of the Establishment and a former Exchange president, had just been jailed for grand larceny. Chairman William O. Douglas of the SEC was angrily breathing down the necks of the Exchange leaders, demanding the abolition of conditions that had resulted in serious trading abuses. Charles R. Gay, who ran the Exchange as president between Whitney and Martin, was in the middle of a continuous battle between two factions in the ruling circle—the floor's Old Guard and its reform element of Young Turks—and unable to make the tough decisions that would set in motion a new course for the organization.

Martin took over this hot seat with a scant business background but with seven years' experience as a commission broker on the floor. A native of St. Louis and the son of a lawyer and local bank president who became head of the Federal Reserve Bank of St. Louis, he had graduated from Yale as an English major in 1928. His first job was at the St. Louis Fed, where he worked for two years as a bank examiner for $67.50 a month. But after hearing through the office grapevine that his career was limited there because of his father's position, he left the bank to join the St. Louis–based brokerage firm of A. G. Edwards & Sons, then owned by relatives, as a statistician.

By 1931 he had become a partner of the firm and shortly thereafter was sent to New York as the head of its eastern operations. In New York he bought his own seat on the Big Board, where he learned how to trade against the speculators and other aggressive traders of that era. He even wrote an article under the name of Martin Maxwell, Jr., in which he said that the Exchange was "one of the most marvelous mechanisms of the machine age." In 1935 he became well known enough to be elected a governor, and when the Conway Committee started to function he was not only appointed secretary of the committee, but was also named chairman of the governing board of the Exchange.

The Conway Committee report, actually drawn up by Martin, began with these words: "While the recommendations herein made would appear to involve a radical alteration of administrative machinery, the necessary changes really represent another step in the long evolutionary development of the Exchange as the nation's primary securities market." It went on from there to recommend a full-time Exchange management, under the leadership of a salaried president who could not be a member of the Exchange, and public representation for the first time on the board of governors. The standing committees, which had long exerted vast power over the affairs of the Big Board, would be sharply reduced in number and superseded by a paid staff, responsible to the president.

Other aspects of the committee report dealt with the Exchange's relationship with Washington, the Big Board's self-regulatory role, and proposals for changes in trading practices. But it was the part concerning the paid administrative staff that became the focus around which the reorganization was based. After much debate, the report was adopted unanimously by the Exchange and Martin sold his Exchange membership to accept the $48,000-a-year post of president that had been unexpectedly offered to him. Edward Everett Bartlett, Jr., a partner of E. A. Pierce & Company who succeeded Martin as chairman of the Exchange, set the tone for the new administration when he said, "The one thing the Exchange has to do now is . . . see that this institution is run for the benefit of the American people."

A serious man whose youth showed beneath his success and the rimless glasses he always wore, Martin did not have the support of all of the Exchange members, despite the overall recognition that reform of the institution was required. "A senior partner of a firm came up to me a while after the election," Martin said many years later, "and told me that he had voted against me because I was too young and just not right for the job. 'Now I want to support you,' he added, 'but would you please buy a hat?' I went out and bought a hat that day."

Martin saw his job as maintaining the integrity of the Exchange so that it could continue its preeminent role in the nation's securities markets. He called the stock market "a savings institution into which the public puts its funds." Wise enough to avoid confrontations with and provocations to the Old Guard, and knowledgeable enough to accept at least some of the programs of the reformers, he attempted to retain and improve the health of the Exchange by keeping it in the middle of the road between federal demands for control and intransigent insistence on no government participation in the market structure. His honesty and good relations with the SEC kept him secure in his position, while his flexibility of mind allowed him to produce the acceptable compromises between the free-enterprise system and the government's indispensable role as a regulator around the edges. "I have no particular objection to government intervention," he remarked. As one account of the period put it, he converted the Big Board "from a private club to a public utility."

Almost immediately, Martin obtained a good press by making himself and the Exchange accessible to the media and the public. Just around the time that he was elected president, the New York Financial Writers Association was established to help develop greater professionalism within the financial journalism fraternity. Martin took the group under his wing, offering support, advice, and criticism when warranted. He believed in an open-door policy and often took his visitors on the floor, even though they were not universally well received there by the membership. Whether on the phone or in person, Martin was relaxed with others and conveyed this attitude of ease and self-confidence to all who were concerned about the welfare of the Exchange.

Martin also quickly put into operation a series of changes designed to improve the Exchange as a marketplace and to offer better protection to public investors. New rules, for example, prohibited member firms from carrying margin accounts for partners or for firms doing business with the public. Firms and their partners and employees were also brought under closer supervision through increased surveillance and reporting requirements.

But Martin could do nothing to stem the malaise on Wall Street based on a paucity of trading during the depression years. Ten years after a membership—with the right to a fractional seat attached to it—on the New York Stock Exchange changed hands for $625,000, the price in 1939 had declined to a low of $51,000. In that year only 20 million shares were traded and the Exchange recorded a loss of more than $1 million as its expenses exceeded its revenues. Even the onset of World War II in 1939 gave just a temporary push to the stock market, which was followed by another slump during and after the fall of France in 1940. Volume continued at a low level into 1941, when the passage of an excess profits tax did nothing to increase interest in the stock market. Early that year, Martin resigned the presidency to be drafted into the Army, and the first period of his influence at the Big Board came to an end. As he said afterward, "I'm not indispensable."

Martin spent four years in the Army, entering as a private and leaving as a colonel. When the war ended, he decided to remain in government service and moved during the next few years through a series of high-level federal posts, including president and chairman of the Export-Import Bank, American executive director of the International Bank for Reconstruction and Development (the World Bank), and Assistant Secretary of the Treasury. It was in the latter position that he became the mediator in a historic clash over the independence of the Federal Reserve System between Treasury Secretary John

W. Snyder and Thomas B. McCabe, chairman of the Federal Reserve Board. Largely due to his ability to bring about an accord between these two strong-willed men, President Harry S Truman, another Missouri Democrat, picked Martin to succeed McCabe as head of the Fed in 1951. "Probably the best appointment Harry Truman ever made," said one Republican senator at the time.

At the Federal Reserve Board, the nation's central bank, Martin was a champion of fiscal conservatism and a symbol of personal rectitude. He earned the sobriquet of "The Happy Puritan" because of his personality and temperament and became an adept mover in the often conflicting worlds of finance and politics. "Money is at the heart and center of a flexible society," he once pointed out. As the country's chief money manager, he was an implacable foe of both inflation and deficit financing. He served as a frequent source of controversy, especially when the economic policies of the Fed did not jibe with the political aims of Presidents and members of Congress. His battles with Representative Wright Patman of Texas over monetary policy were legendary.

During his tenure of almost nineteen years as chairman of the FRB, Martin's actions in tightening and loosening the nation's money supply often directly and indirectly influenced stock prices on the New York exchange. In addition, he made a speech during the economic boom in 1965 in which he sounded a pointed warning against stock market excesses that could repeat the cycle of boom and bust that led to the 1929 depression. Using words that shocked the nation and brought upon him the wrath of President Lyndon B. Johnson for being a Cassandra, Martin said:

> We find disquieting similarities between our present prosperity and the fabulous twenties. . . . When economic pressures are at their brightest, the dangers of complacency and recklessness are greatest. . . . If monetary history were to repeat itself, it would be nobody's fault but our own.

The stock market plunged sharply on these words—the Dow Jones Industrial Index alone skidded nineteen points in three days—and Martin's former colleagues at the Big Board were more than a little upset at the man who once was the leading representative of their interests. But Martin stuck to his guns, observing that "there is nothing in the speech that I want to change."

In 1970 Martin retired from the Federal Reserve Board and prepared to devote himself to a more relaxed retirement life that included directorships of a number of such major corporations as U. S. Steel and IBM and a consultancy to the Riggs National Bank in Washington, D.C. But a year later, at the age of sixty-four, he was once again called upon by the New York Stock Exchange to fulfill an important role, and once again he accepted. The request was to undertake, without compensation, a searching examination of the Exchange's structure, rules, and procedures in a new effort at reforming the institution after a devastating period of financial distress for Wall Street. The London *Times* likened his recall to service at the Big Board to a Western movie in which a gunfighter returns home to save the town from ruthless cattle barons.

"The public interest is the paramount interest," Martin said as he stepped into harness once more at 11 Wall Street. "I really didn't want this job. I guess what led me to say 'yes' was my Puritan concern that it was a job that needed doing and it would be a good thing for me to do it."

Martin began his task with an open and obvious bias in favor of Wall Street and the auction market of securities exchanges. "It is vital to the growth and development of this country that we have a securities market—and a central securities market is a vital and necessary thing—that we can trust," he noted. "I'm a believer in pure competition. There should be losses occasionally, as well as profits, in a free-enterprise society."

Martin, who knew the Big Board inside and out, investigated the workings of the Exchange for five months, backed by an advisory committee of industry bigwigs. At the conclusion, he issued a major report in 1971 that called for a substantial reorganization of the New York exchange, as well as a reordering of all the country's stock exchanges into a national market system. While the national market could not be established independently by the New York Stock Exchange, the internal restructuring called for in the penetrating and controversial report could be done immediately. "This reorganization should proceed promptly and not await formation of the proposed national exchange system," Martin said.

The result was that although the recommendations were not binding, the Exchange responded by adopting a corporate form and becoming the New York Stock Exchange, Inc. The thirty-three-man board of governors then existing was supplanted by a twenty-one-member board of directors. Ten of these directors were elected from the securities industry, ten were elected from the public sector outside of the Exchange community, and one was the paid, full-time chairman named by the other directors. Thus the chairman had become an administrative official with no ties to any member firms and loyal only to the Exchange itself, rather than a part-time officer who shared responsibility with the paid president.

"I could have gone back to the New York Stock Exchange as the chairman," Martin said later, after many provisions of the comprehensive Martin Report had been adopted and the Exchange was launched on a new path. "But I didn't want to do that anymore. You know, I came out of college believing that the New York Stock Exchange was the greatest free enterprise in the world. I still have a great affection for it and I'd hate to see it put under because of the mistakes and miscalculations of some of its people."

EMIL SCHRAM:
A HOOSIER
FROM WASHINGTON

When Bill Martin resigned the presidency of the New York Stock Exchange in 1941 to join the Army, he recommended to the board of governors that his successor be someone intimately familiar with the intricacies of the securities markets. The board, however, thought differently and hired a man with a Washington background and contacts, but with no direct Wall Street experience. "I have nothing to say," said Private Martin when contacted by the press at his basic training camp.

The man selected as the next paid president of the Big Board was Emil Schram, chairman of the Reconstruction Finance Corporation (RFC) and a farmer from Peru, Indiana. A close associate and protégé of Jesse Jones, one of the leading New Dealers in the Roosevelt administration and at that time Secretary of Commerce, Schram was an able executive who quickly learned what the Exchange was all about and went on to develop programs and policies to move it successfully through the years of World War II and immediately afterward. During his regime, though, a cabal came together to demand a return to the powerful committee structure that had existed before the reforms of 1938. Schram not only bested this group, but also pushed through still further reforms that

ensured the centralization of Exchange management under a paid executive staff headed by the president.

"I came in at a time of change, when a younger generation had taken over on the floor," Schram recalled almost
four decades after stepping into the position. "They
offered the job to several old-timers on Wall Street who
turned it down, so then they finally called me. I was the
first outsider."

Schram was called in from the outside because the
leaders on the floor of the Exchange perceived their principal need was to maintain good relations with the federal
government. The governors and their associates felt per-
fectly capable of keeping the floor operating according to
the principles and standards of that era. But they wanted
someone in their corner who would have links to Washington and would be their buffer when the pressures from
that direction became too severe. This they found in
Schram.

A third-generation descendent of a family of German
immigrants, Schram was born in 1893 and ended his formal education at the high school level. His first job was in
the office of a coal and timber dealer in Peru, the small
Indiana town where he lived. The dealer was impressed
by Schram's native ability and gave him the responsibility
of draining and developing a five-thousand-acre tract of
swampy land on the banks of the Illinois River.

At the point that he was given this task, Schram knew
nothing about either farming or irrigation. But he was a
quick study and before too long drained and planted the
land, which became a thriving and productive midwest-
ern farm. Over the years, Schram became an expert in the
drainage field and was elected chairman of the National
Drainage Association. In this capacity, he met Jesse

Jones, the first chairman of the New Deal's RFC—one of the key federal lending agencies established by President Franklin D. Roosevelt. Jones brought him to Washington in 1933, where his first position was chief of the agency's drainage, levee, and irrigation division.

Schram moved up in the RFC hierarchy to the board of directors in 1936 and succeeded Jones to the chairmanship in 1939. He also took on directorships in other federal agencies concerned with providing funds to stimulate different areas of the economy. Early in 1941 he moved into an even more sensitive spot when he was named assistant director of the priorities division of the Office of Production Management. Nevertheless, he decided that the time had come for him, at the age of forty-eight, to seek out employment providing greater financial security in the private sector.

With his mentor Jones providing the moral support for his job search ("I know you want to get out of here," Jones said), Schram was put in contact with the Big Board committee seeking a successor to Martin. No promises were made by Schram about utilizing his Washington contacts, but it was clear that the board of governors expected to derive some value from his government service. "It rather intrigued me because the New York Stock Exchange is an institution almost as old as the U.S. government," Schram reported. "But I said that I did not have any influence in Washington, and if I did, it would not be for sale."

Yet the nominating committee thought in different terms about Schram's role—considering it to a large extent to be a liaison with the regulators of the securities industry—and unanimously voted to recommend that the directors appoint him to the $48,000-a-year position. (By the time he left in 1951, the salary had been raised to $100,000.) And Jones was effusive in his praise: "The governors of the New York Stock Exchange are to be congratulated upon securing the services of Emil Schram as president of that important institution. . . . He is unusually capable and well-qualified for this position of great trust. All of us in government will miss Emil."

Right from the outset, Schram showed that he was perspicacious enough to deal with the shrewd traders and brokers on the floor who comprised the bulk of his membership. Admittedly he was not an authority on the machinery of the Exchange, or Wall Street itself for that matter. But he understood management and knew how to work with and through people—a characteristic that augmented his government service in determining his value to the Big Board.

As a condition of employment, he insisted that a number of administrative reforms be made to heighten Exchange efficiency, and these were approved soon after Schram was officially inducted on July 1, 1941. (On that day, incidentally, he had to ask a cabdriver where the Exchange building was located, since he had never been there before.) Among the powers that Schram sought were that the remaining segments of the discredited standing committee system for running the Exchange (which Martin had largely abolished on the recommendation of the Conway Committee) be finally eliminated and that the size of the board of governors be cut from thirty-three to a more workable level of twenty-five members. In addition, he asked that the nominating committee be empowered to name a successor committee, none of whom could be governors, as well as a slate of candidates for the board. All of these recommendations were adopted.

Schram also took pains to make sure that the president's office at the Big Board had the authority he deemed necessary for full control. A letter to the membership stating the outlines of the reorganization made this point crystal clear:

> The president would be the chief executive officer of the Exchange. He would represent the Exchange in all public matters and in relations with the government and its agencies. He would be responsible for the management and administration of the Exchange. . . . The president would be responsible, through such organization machinery as he may set up, for the selection of all employees, for their direction, for fixing the terms and conditions of their employment. . . . The responsibility for the relations between the Exchange and the public belongs necessarily and obviously to the president and his professional advisers.

With this formal statement of his responsibility, Schram felt that he had a clear mandate to speak for the New York Stock Exchange in keeping with the policies established by the board of governors. And he was readily accepted by the floor on the one hand and by the upstairs commission brokers on the other.

"I was there at a pretty tough time," he said, "because we were still recovering from the big crash. Most of the traders were in debt to the government for taxes from profits they had made in the past. You had to hold stocks three years then to get the capital gains rate, and I spent a lot of time in Washington before convincing Congress to change it to a six-month holding period and maximum 25 percent tax."

After the United States entered World War II, rumors constantly cropped up on the floor that President Roosevelt would close the Exchange, just as it had been closed for periods in 1873 and 1914. Schram went down to Washington in 1943 to see if he could ascertain the government's plans and convince the Administration not to try to force a shutdown.

"The President invited me for lunch at his desk of chicken à la king and stewed peaches," Schram said. "He told me about his trip to the Casablanca Conference and he talked a lot about his boys. And he told me that Henry Morgenthau [Secretary of the Treasury] and Marriner Eccles [Chairman of the Federal Reserve Board] urged him to shut down the Exchange for the duration of the war.

"I said to him that only the governors have the authority to shut the Exchange and asked him not to take any action. I explained that private financing was necessary for the war effort and that this financing would be affected by a shutdown. Roosevelt then recalled that his old New York law firm was the outside counsel for the Exchange and told me he wouldn't close it. 'But promise me you'll watch it closely and, if you see it running into trouble, you'll tell me immediately,' he said. And that's how close the Exchange came to being closed."

Schram kept the Exchange open, but he also had to cope with extremely distressed conditions on the floor during the wartime years. In 1942 there were just 537 member firms, compared with 665 before the crash of 1929. Only 6,700 securities salesmen, also known as customers' men or registered representatives, were in the field to hustle for business in 1942, a fraction of the number from decades past. The price of a seat on the floor that year plummeted to a twentieth-century low of $17,000, while the total market value of all listed shares was just $38.8 billion. The turnover—or ratio of listed shares to volume—was only 9 percent, compared with 119 percent in 1929 and a whopping 319 percent in 1901. Many of the traders and customers had gone off to war, and much of the profits from the brokerage business went off with them.

"I knew the fellow who bought that seat for $17,000," Schram later observed. "He was a Scotsman who said he bought it because he had confidence in the Exchange. When someone said to him that it was a pretty bad price, he replied, 'But think of what it would be without Schram.' By the way, he sold out in 1944 for $75,000 and told me, 'Emil, it's not because I lost confidence in you. It's just that it's too nice a profit.'"

Also part of his program for increasing volume for the floor in those dark days was Schram's espousal of a new trading mechanism: the special offering. Special offerings allowed sellers of large blocks of stock to dispose of them on the floor without depressing the price by allowing buyers to be brought together who would purchase the securities in a special transaction at a less-than-market price. Schram convinced the SEC to approve this measure, and although it did not cause a radical upsurge in trading, it did bring some additional revenues to the floor.

Schram was indefatigable as he traveled to the legislatures in Washington and Albany and crisscrossed the country to speak on behalf of the Exchange and its place in the nation's economic system. While many federal officials never did understand how the Exchange structure functioned, Schram—who started with little or no knowledge on this subject himself—became an expert who took the time and trouble to explain new developments to others. He worked well with wartime chairmen Robert Stott and John A. Coleman, both self-made men like himself who reached the pinnacle of the Exchange power structure by their wits rather than their family connections. And he kept the Exchange apparatus intact until prices started picking up toward the end of the war.

The last major wartime crisis for Schram and the Exchange occurred in 1945 when President Roosevelt died suddenly at his retreat in Warm Springs, Georgia. "I was having dinner that night in the Links Club when John Coleman called and said there would be a special board meeting immediately," Schram said. "We received a message from Secretary Morgenthau that the Treasury would support the government bond market and that we should stay open. So I rang the bell the next morning at 10 A.M. and we had a strong market all day."

During the immediate postwar years, Schram lost some of his vigor, although he continued to enjoy the support of the floor and the board of governors. A wise leader who never ran too far ahead of his troops, he anticipated their desires to obtain more volume and to sell the virtues of the free-enterprise system—and devoted many hours to a public relations campaign promoting the Exchange as the center of the capitalistic system. And for the most part, he kept the then faltering Securities and Exchange Commission at bay.

In 1948, however, a dissident group on the floor mounted a campaign against him in an attempt to reduce the power of the board of governors and return to the committee system of organization. The group wanted not only a lesser role for the nonmember officers like Schram, but also the reestablishment of a larger board, like the one that existed before Schram took office, in which the floor would have more authority. Schram immediately charged that the committee system was the "method of management which created in the public mind the impression that the institution was conducted as a private club." And he asserted that the entire movement was no more than "talk among a discontented element of the membership calculated to create the impression that the governors are in some way divided in their sense of responsibility to the institution." Within a year, the rump group disintegrated and all of its proposals but one were forgotten—in 1950 the board size was increased back to thirty-three. Yet the long, grueling effort to defeat this move took its toll on Schram.

For in 1949 Schram suffered a heart attack and was away from his desk for eight months. When he returned, he made the decision to leave the Exchange, recognizing that the pressures that affected his body once could very easily affect it again, and told the board in 1950 that he wished to resign. Not with pleasure, but with the realization of its necessity, the governors accepted his resignation, offered him a $25,000-a-year pension, and began anew the search for a successor. They also flooded the press with accolades to their departing chieftain and held the traditional farewell testimonial dinner in his honor.

As for Schram, he returned to his Indiana farm, where he had previously spent many years amid his acres of corn and wheat and hogs. Schram could point with pride to his accomplishments in increasing the funds in the Exchange treasury from $3 million when he arrived to $15 million when he left ten years later. He never forgot the

Big Board, moreover, and decades later the memories of the people on the floor were as lucid as ever in his mind. "There's no place in the world where the hopes and fears of the American people are expressed as clearly as they are on the floor of the New York Stock Exchange," he said. "We certainly need it today as much as we ever did."

9 G. KEITH FUNSTON:
THE RIGHT MAN
FOR THE RIGHT TIME

When G. Keith Funston became president of the New York Stock Exchange on May 24, 1951, it formally symbolized the end of the last traces of the Richard Whitney era. For Funston was a poor boy who pulled himself up by his bootstraps to achieve what is one of the most, if not the most, prestigious positions in the American business world. And unlike Whitney, who was to the manner born, the six-foot, three-inch Funston did it by dint of his personality and his salesmanship—not his money in the bank.

Funston, moreover, had the good fortune to be at the helm of the Big Board when the post–World War II bull market was at its greatest flourishing. At the beginning of 1951 the bellwether Dow Jones Industrial Average—the index that most people consider the best barometer of stock market activity—stood at 239.92. By the end of 1967, when Funston's tour as president had come to an end, the Dow closed at 905.11.

No one, not even the man himself, would give Funston all of the credit for pushing the stock market up to what was then a new high. But the optimistic tone that he infused within the Wall Street community with his resonant voice and cheerful demeanor, coupled with his successful "Own Your Share of American Business" campaign, which sharply increased the number of stockholders, certainly played an important part in creating the climate for this upsurge to occur. Ever the evangelist, peppering his speech with "gee," "gosh," and "by golly," Funston believed in capitalism, knew how to market its theory and practice, and helped the members of the New York exchange prosper from the greater public interest in buying common stocks.

While he was selling shares of American business, Funston was also minding the store—in his case, the Big Board. The historic split between the floor members and the upstairs members who dealt directly with the public still existed, but now the upstairs firms were demanding more of a voice in the management of the New York Stock Exchange. Their surging sales led to a greater assertiveness within the ruling councils of the Exchange and less of a willingness to take a back seat to the floor in determining policy and charting future growth.

"It used to be that the chairman [then the top non-paid Exchange position to which a member was elected] would always come from the floor," Funston recalled. "We changed that so that the chairman would alternate between the floor and upstairs."

Funston also tried to bring more upstairs members into the active workings of the hierarchy by changing the time of the board of governors' meetings. Stock market trading then ended at 3 P.M., and meetings were scheduled at 3:15 P.M. to meet the convenience of the floor members. But the upstairs members—particularly those from firms headquartered outside of New York—would often be anxious to leave soon thereafter, so that an air of impatience hung over the boardroom as the meeting progressed. Sometimes matters would be rushed through to accommodate the clock and not receive as much or as thorough attention as they would if they had been taken up at an earlier hour.

"I told the floor, 'People go on vacations. Why not take one day off a month?'" Funston said. "But I lost this one." Actually Funston lost the battle but won the war, since the board later reversed itself and agreed to start the meetings earlier and allow more time for discussion.

Funston lasted as long as he did in the hot seat at the Exchange partly because of his ability to accommodate himself to all of the groups at the Exchange and to help them come up with a decision. He would compromise if necessary, but he wound up with a decision that everyone would back. "Nothing is black and white," he pointed out. "Some member-firm people say that the floor runs everything and that the floor members are a bunch of Neanderthals. But that's a lot of bunk. It's just that the floor sells its viewpoint a lot better than member firms do. At the Exchange, you know, the floor is the production department and the upstairs firms are the sales department."

Funston achieved his goal of bringing the floor and the upstairs members together on many issues by moving slowly and constantly striving for gradual, rather than radical, changes. "Not many people realized it was happening," he noted. "If they did, they would have resented it."

Reaching the pinnacle at the Exchange—and earning the respect of both the floor and non-floor members—was quite an achievement for George Keith Funston, born in Waterloo, Iowa, in 1910, the son of a dentist who moved the family to Sioux Falls, South Dakota. Funston's boyhood was filled with remembrances of the different jobs held by his father. Dr. George E. Funston became a banker until a panic in the 1920s put an end to his banks, and he later turned into an insurance salesman and a United States Department of Agriculture official. Through it all, his only son—whom everyone called Keith, his mother's maiden name—went to local schools and worked part-time candling eggs in a grocery store, helping out in a packing plant, and running errands for a bank.

After graduating from high school in 1932, Funston decided, at the urging of his bishop, to accept a scholarship to Trinity College in Hartford, Connecticut—a decision that played a major role in determining the course of his life. For, while a student there, he helped earn his tuition by serving as a chauffeur to the president, Remson B. Ogilby. And twelve years later, at the age of thirty-four, Funston became one of the youngest college presidents in the country when he succeeded Ogilby as the head of the prestigious New England Episcopal liberal arts school.

In the years between his graduation from Trinity as class valedictorian and his triumphal return there as its head, Funston earned a master of business administration degree from the Harvard Business School and worked as a junior executive for the American Radiator and Standard Sanitary Corporation and Sylvania Electric Products, Inc. Just before the United States entered World War II, he went into government service as a dollar-a-year man at the War Production Board.

During his three years in Washington, Funston charmed both industrialists and politicians as a special assistant first to Sidney J. Weinberg, deputy chairman of the board, and then to Donald M. Nelson, its chairman. His contacts with Weinberg were the spur that brought him to Wall Street years later, however, since Weinberg was the legendary senior partner of Goldman, Sachs & Co. and long one of the key members of the Wall Street establishment. And when Weinberg recommended Funston for the top position at the New York Stock Exchange, the job was his for the asking.

Before assuming the post as the official voice of the nation's leading financial market, Funston spent two years as a lieutenant commander in the Navy and seven years as the president of his alma mater, during which time he raised the value of its plant and endowments by 50 percent. All of this was a prologue to the sixteen-year period at the Big Board when his name became synonymous with capitalism—or, as he liked to put it, "people's capitalism." Named to succeed the ailing Emil Schram from a list of over one hundred candidates as the Exchange's paid president, he quickly built up an effective, hardworking staff and a loyal following among the membership.

Not too long after Funston joined the New York Stock Exchange at an initial salary of $100,000 a year, he developed the concept and the tag line "Own Your Share of American Business." As he said, "I'll try to be a salesman of shares in America." With his tenure at the Exchange coinciding with a wide-scale interest in investing, Funston was in the right place at the right time as millions of Americans entered the stock market and became participants in the game of investing. One Wall Streeter of that day observed, "Keith has always been a 'follow me' kind of guy."

Of course, Funston recognized—if for no other reason than the self-interest of the Exchange—that inexperienced speculators could be financially ruined in the market. And so he always issued a caveat of some sort in his speeches or interviews that extolled the virtues of investing in listed securities on the New York Stock Exchange.

"We have never said that *everybody* in the United States ought to own stock," he once said in an interview. "Our function is to call attention to the opportunity to invest *provided* that the person gets the facts from reputable brokers and *provided* that he most certainly does not operate on hot tips. As experienced investors have long known, neither low prices nor new issues are guarantees of anything except, perhaps, a proportionately greater degree of risk.

"The reason we sound these cautions is because we care. We care because people can get hurt. It's not just altruism on our part. We know that if there's a lot of dangerous amateur speculation, there will be a lot of disillusionment. And even though they may not buy from our members, they'll blame it on us."

Funston was the man responsible for creating the Monthly Investment Plan method of investing, which for a while became the rage on Wall Street. Individuals could invest in a particular security for as little as forty dollars every quarter through a procedure whereby they could purchase either full or partial shares. At the height of the Funston era, it seemed that "everyone" wanted to own stock and talk about his or her exploits in the market.

The success of Funston's efforts during this "golden age" for the Exchange in balancing altruism with friendly persuasion can be seen in the rise in American shareowners, as measured by the New York Stock Exchange's stockholder census. The list of men and women who owned a share of American business grew from 6.5 million in 1952, the year after Funston took office, to 30.8 million in 1970, just a few years after he left. As recognized by the Exchange board of governors through public tributes and financial remuneration, much of the rise was due to Funston's proselytizing throughout the country on behalf of the floor of the Exchange and all that it represented. Funston himself described his efforts in this fashion: "In order to be successful, you must look successful."

Whatever his successes in selling the Exchange and its products—many of which have never been equaled by his successors—Funston's finest hour occurred in an entirely different, and less pleasant, set of circumstances. In November 1963, during the same weekend that the nation mourned the assassination of President Kennedy, Ira Haupt & Co., a venerable and important member firm on the Big Board, was suspended as a result of the Great Salad Oil Scandal. Allied Crude Vegetable Oil Refining Company—Haupt's largest commodity customer, which had engaged in fraudulent sales of nonexistent salad oil by means of phony warehouse receipts—was unable to meet $18 million worth of margin calls. As a result, Haupt was plunged into a deficit position.

Funston, who was suffering from a bad cold, worked around the clock to supervise the liquidation of Haupt, to advance up to $12 million in stock exchange funds to help free customer securities and cash balances, and to establish a special trust fund for possible use in future insolvencies. This task required an equal measure of force and tact, as Funston had to wrest last-minute agreements in one of the most confusing situations ever to hit the financial community from partners of the firm, creditors, and lawyers representing all parties in the matter. With characteristic modesty, Funston simply said, "There was a lot of gut fighting."

A few years later, with Funston almost fifty-seven years

old and still active, he felt the time had come for him to bid farewell to the Big Board in order to pursue other challenges and interests. So he gave more than a year's notice to the board of governors and lined up about a dozen corporate directorships—"These concerns were anxious to get a different viewpoint and I think I supplied one"—that would keep him as busy as he wanted to be. Funston left the Exchange as its leader for the last time on September 8, 1967, and moved out into a different part of the business world. Before departing, though, he made an unusual appearance on the rostrum above the trading floor to ring the gong signaling the close of trading, to be greeted by loud applause and the singing by the membership of their traditional song of nostalgia, "Wait 'Til the Sun Shines, Nellie."

After leaving the Exchange, Funston spent four and a half years as the part-time chairman of the Olin Corporation, along with his other directorships. He was also besieged by offers to write a book about his reflections and experiences on Wall Street—offers that continue to this day. But Funston had no desire to present an insider's view of the workings of the Exchange he ran because of his desire to retain the respect and friendship of those he worked with over the years.

"When I came to the Exchange, I had no idea I would stay this long," he said afterward. "The early days—the first year or two—were the roughest. The securities business was bad, seat prices were down, I was getting established in my job and with the board of governors. But there was never a moment when I didn't feel completely sure of myself and the job."

ROBERT W. HAACK:
A BROKER
AT THE HELM

President Franklin D. Roosevelt is said to have called the presidency of the New York Stock Exchange "the second toughest job in the world," and Robert W. Haack, a trim six-footer with graying dark hair, is certainly one man who must agree with that description. For the five years of Haack's tenure as head of the Big Board were probably among the toughest in the entire history of the Exchange.

During this period, Haack was faced with a series of crises on Wall Street: an enormous paper-work crunch in the back offices of member firms; the liquidation or merger of respected, old-line houses, which threatened the collapse of others; and the realization that many brokerage and investment banking concerns would become publicly owned for the first time. In addition, one of the Exchange's oldest traditions—the fixed commission rate for all brokerage transactions—was also moving toward abolishment, despite the efforts of the financial community's Old Guard to restrain this movement.

It was this issue of fixed, or nonnegotiated, commissions, moreover, that for a time set Haack against the board of governors that had hired him. Eventually the board approved the unfixing of rates just as Haack had recommended, but not until there had been a series of heavy Wall Street shock waves over the plan.

Much later, Haack recalled, "Members came up to me and said, 'If we had listened to you and not had to have it rammed down our throats by the SEC, we would have the national market system at 11 Wall Street [headquarters of the New York Stock Exchange].' But the fall-out was that the proposal later brought out of the closet some of the more forward-looking people on the Street who supported me in this effort."

At the time that Haack broke his silence over this subject, however, there were few, if any, expressions of support from the power structure at the Exchange. "The policy of the New York Stock Exchange is made by the board of governors, not the president," said Bernard J. Lasker, chairman of the board. There were even some calls for his resignation from the floor because of what was considered by the members to be an act of heresy. But Haack weathered this storm and went on to conclude his five-year term of office and win back the support of most of his detractors.

Every head of the Big Board reached this pinnacle via a different route, but Haack's was probably the most direct since his entire business career had been in the securities industry. The son of an insurance agent for the Mutual Life Insurance Company of New York—of which Bob Haack is now a trustee—he was born in a small town near Milwaukee, Wisconsin, in 1917. After graduating as a scholarship student from the Harvard Graduate School of Business in 1940, he was hired as a $125-a-month securities analyst by the Wisconsin Company, a Milwaukee brokerage firm that later changed its name to Robert W. Baird & Co.

Haack enlisted in the Navy shortly after Pearl Harbor and served in the South Pacific as a pilot. In 1945 he returned to Baird, where he spent the next nineteen years at a variety of jobs, including manager of the trading department, syndicate manager, institutional sales manager, and partner. "I did just about everything at that firm," Haack observed long afterward.

As he rose through the ranks at his own company, Haack also became involved in the activities of the National Association of Securities Dealers (NASD), the quasi-official self-regulatory organization of the four thousand securities dealers in the over-the-counter market. Over-the-counter stocks are those that are not listed on a securities exchange—and the trading of these stocks had long had a less than savory reputation. The Securities and Exchange Commission investigated this market and, following a one-year study, concluded that the NASD had "fallen short of its potential as a self-regulatory agency." The commission stung the over-the-counter dealers by calling for a general tightening of discipline over NASD members, more efficient surveillance of trading activities, and higher requirements for membership.

Haack was aware of these deficiencies and tried to help change the image of the over-the-counter market and its watchdog action committees by working within the NASD to bring about reform. In 1961 he became a member of the association's board of directors and in 1964 was elected its chairman. Within a few months, the NASD decided to establish a full-time administrative position of president of the association, and the $80,000-a-year job was offered to Haack. After deliberating for five weeks, he resigned his Baird partnership and accepted the new challenge. "We were delighted that he considered it because it was quite a step down [financially] from his Baird partnership," said one leader of the organization.

"I don't want to sound like Sir Galahad," Haack said shortly after moving to the association's headquarters in Washington, D.C. "But I came down here because I believe in the SEC study. If it were not for the study group's recommendations and my belief that self-regulation needs a businessman's viewpoint too, I doubt that I would have come."

At the NASD, Haack quickly took charge. He forced over-the-counter dealers to list the actual, rather than unrealistic, spreads between bid and asked prices, so that customers would be better informed. He put the wheels in motion for the establishment of the NASDAQ automated quotation system for over-the-counter stocks. In all, he pushed through a majority of the seventy-five reforms that the SEC wanted. "He was a breath of fresh air in a dank hall," said one leading Wall Street executive.

Haack's successes at the NASD did not escape the attention of the power structure at the New York Stock Exchange, then seeking a successor to G. Keith Funston, who had announced his retirement in 1966. Admittedly Haack was not the first choice for the Big Board job. The governors initially wanted Donald C. Cook, president of the American Electric Power Company, but Cook would not accept without assurances that he would have greater authority than the Exchange was willing to give. The board next turned to Haack with an offer for a five-year, $125,000-a-year contract, and in 1967, at the age of fifty-six, Haack assumed the presidency. "He is superbly qualified for this position of leadership," asserted Walter

N. Frank, one of the best-known specialists on the floor and then chairman of the Big Board.

Qualified as he was, Haack was immediately enmeshed in a slew of bread-and-butter issues affecting the floor of the Exchange. Initially one stood out above the others: the system's inability to handle efficiently a continued high level of trading volume. Daily average turnover in the years immediately after his election was between 10 million and 13 million shares a day—a fraction of the average trading within the next decade—but the member firms were nevertheless swamped in a sea of paper work. There were mix-ups in transactions, stock certificates were lost, and the clearing of securities was uneven. To reduce this overload, Haack recommended first that the closing time of the Exchange be pushed up an hour a day and then that the Exchange floor be closed completely on Wednesday. Eventually the computers at most of the member organizations caught up with the backlog and the floor was able to return to a full five-day week. But Haack was on the go all the time and observed, "I sometimes feel as though I'm playing center field with ten people hitting fly balls to me at one time."

The Haack years also saw, however, the end of some well-known, venerable member firms that could not make it through the confusion and turmoil of the late 1960s and early 1970s. Despite his best efforts, McDonnell & Co. and Dempsey-Tegler & Co. went under when their liabilities far exceeded their assets. Hayden, Stone & Co., Goodbody & Co., and Francis I. DuPont & Co. all had rescue operations in which their assets were acquired by other firms, while their liabilities were more or less assumed by the other members of the Exchange. Smaller and lesser-known firms were also dissolved.

"Just keeping the thing afloat was an accomplishment," Haack would later say about those turbulent days on and off the floor. "We were putting out fires all the time." But always the optimist, he added, "If marginal units are weeded out, services extended, and costs reduced, the public itself will be the beneficiary."

For most of Haack's tenure, he was generally popular among the membership, particularly among the professionals on the floor. "My door was open and people would sometimes come up and bitch," he said. "But I tried to lobby some of the leaders on the floor. I had been a trader, a market maker, and an arbitrageur, and I had pretty good rapport with them. I personally knew the agony and the ecstasy of being long and short at the same time. And I told them that until someone generates an order they don't come into play."

Haack's popularity stood him in good stead when the tenuous unity of the Exchange was threatened as a trend spread toward encouraging member firms to become publicly owned. When Donaldson, Lufkin & Jenrette—the first member firm to announce that it would make a public offering—was finalizing its plans, the ranks of Wall Street were solidly closed behind the official position that the capital of securities firms must remain in private hands to guarantee the long-term solidity and integrity of the industry. But before too long a time had passed, Haack managed to convince the board of governors that the inevitable "going public" trend could not be stopped, and it went along with his recommendation to remove all such restrictions. Today many of the major firms have part of their ownership in the hands of outside stockholders.

"Permitting public ownership of equity securities issued by member firms can open the way to an infusion of badly needed capital," Haack argued. These arguments proved to be an augury of things to come a decade later when, even with public ownership, there was insufficient capital at many firms to cope with the demands of securities trading in a changed market environment.

For Haack, though, the most difficult period of his reign at the New York Stock Exchange came when he took a giant step forward toward the abolition of the sacred fixed commission rate for brokerage transactions on and off the floor. Although nonnegotiated sales commissions had been a watchword of the Exchange since the Buttonwood Agreement of 1792, pressure was building up from Congress and the SEC to begin testing the efficacy of negotiating the commission charges paid to buy and sell securities. Particularly desired by the Washington regulators were the development of volume discounts to institutional customers like mutual funds and the elimination of "give-ups," whereby the broker receiving the sales commission shares it with others designated by the institution. But the board of governors, reflecting the attitude of the membership, was adamant against deviating from its historic policy of one fixed price for everyone.

Traditionally the president of the Exchange gave voice to and implemented board policy, and initially Haack was a vehement supporter of fixed rates. Even before officially assuming the office, he contended that "the give-up and the lead broker concept are the most economical and efficient ways to handle an institutional order, certainly more practical than parceling out two thousand shares each to twenty-five different brokers with all the phoning, servicing, deliveries, and payments that would go along with it." In his first public address as president in 1967, he said that the public interest is not "necessarily served by a reduction in fees or charges resulting in a securities industry which is less healthy and less able to serve the public interest." And the following year he told the SEC that abolishing minimum rates would cripple the Big Board, with damaging consequences to investors.

But by 1970 he had become convinced that this time-honored practice of the securities industry would soon have to come to an end—if for no other reason than the industry's own best interests. And so on November 17 of that year, in an openly critical speech before the prestigious Economic Club of New York—a speech that he specifically noted did "not necessarily represent the views of the board of governors"—Haack shocked the industry by stating: "Notwithstanding my own previous personal and strong support of fixed minimum commissions, I believe that it now behooves our industry leaders to rethink their personal judgments on negotiated rates. While I question whether or not the industry is presently sufficiently strong financially to completely disregard fixed minimum rates, I personally think it might well consider full negotiated commissions as an ultimate objective."

The reaction to this unorthodox view about a supersensitive issue was as swift as it was strong. Hardly had the morning papers been read before denunciations poured forth from Exchange officials. Judging from their consternation, it was almost as if a spy had been discovered in their ranks. As it turned out, these comments were all unnecessary, since within six months the first moves toward negotiated rates were taken by those very same governors —steps that led to fully negotiated rates on May 1, 1975.

"My speech was probably born out of frustration as

much as anything else," Haack said afterward. "Everybody was pursuing their own financial interests, which didn't always coincide with others' financial interests. One of the purposes of that exercise was to get the sparks flying. It was really not the hard-line speech that it was reported to be. My motivation was the continuation of this market and its improvement. I had to decide whether to be a lordly executive or a working stiff. I chose the latter and haven't regretted it."

Less than a year after delivering the controversial address that brought him and his views to the attention of the man on the street—although Haack declared that he had no desire to become a household name—he told the board that he would not renew his contract when it expired in 1972. He wanted to become a professional director, out of the pressure cooker and public spotlight, with no full-time administrative ties to any corporation. He soon added memberships on the boards of the Lockheed Corporation, Merrill Lynch, Nabisco, Libbey-Owens-Ford, and Marsh & McLennan to that of Mutual of New York. "I'm tired of being in the middle of a fight," he said.

Ironically, Haack was right back in the middle less than four years later. Lockheed became torn apart by an escalating scandal involving payoffs to foreign governments, and its chairman, Daniel J. Haughton, was forced to step down. Haack was drafted by his fellow directors for that hot seat in 1975 and did the required job of restoring Lockheed's credibility and reorganizing its management in his typical mild-mannered style. Although he had no previous experience as an industrial manager, he reduced the company's enormous debt and negotiated a new private financing at much better terms. With that task completed, Haack retired from the ranks of full-time management for a second time.

Of all his myriad business experiences in and out of the securities industry, Haack looks back on his years at the New York Stock Exchange and his relationships with its members as the most significant. "The floor is functioning pretty well," he said. "A younger group of people there today have a touch of vision that some of their fathers didn't have. These people see the light of day in a very meaningful, public-spirited way. The floor is the most vulnerable part of the whole operation, but it's still the best thing around."

11 JAMES J. NEEDHAM: FIGHTING FOR THE FLOOR AND WITH IT

If anyone recognizes the power of the floor members of the New York Stock Exchange today vis-à-vis the upstairs members who act as agents for their customers, it is James J. Needham. For Needham, who served as chairman and chief executive officer of the Big Board from 1972 to 1976, was forced to resign from what is probably the most visible post on Wall Street principally because the floor had lost confidence in his ability to represent its interests.

Actually, Needham never envisioned his job as working for the interests of any single group within the membership of the Exchange. He spoke of representing the entire Exchange community and of even going beyond that to ensure that the public interest was best served by any actions taken on behalf of the Big Board. But during his tenure at the Exchange he came to understand the conflicting viewpoints within his constituency and watched as the floor members fought for the control that they thought had been unjustly taken away from them.

The story of Needham's incumbency is the story of the floor's battle to regain the position of supremacy it long enjoyed until the reorganization of the Exchange in 1972. And it indicates how difficult it is to change long-lasting institutional patterns, despite the desire of the governing body and the even greater desire of Congress and the Securities and Exchange Commission to do so.

In 1971 the Exchange had asked William McChesney Martin, Jr., a former president of the Big Board, to recommend a reorganization plan that would result in better controls over the financial malpractices exposed by the previous two years' massive bear market. Martin was brought in for this job essentially because confidence in the Exchange had been severely shaken as more than 100 of the 630 member firms disappeared through merger or liquidation.

The Martin Report turned out to be an extensive document that not only recommended changes in the organization of the New York Stock Exchange, but also sought a sweeping reorganization of the nation's securities markets. The report for the first time called for a national market system whereby the New York Stock Exchange, the American Stock Exchange, the regional stock exchanges, and the over-the-counter market would be linked into a single, central auction market.

This central market could not be implemented by the Big Board on its own, but the recommendations affecting the New York exchange could be adopted unilaterally. The most significant of these recommendations was put into effect, therefore, in 1972: a changeover from a thirty-three-man board of governors composed largely of individuals in the securities industry, with heavy representation from the floor, to a twenty-one-man board of directors with ten persons from the industry (of which just three are from the floor) and ten representing the public. The twenty-first director would be the chairman, a paid, full-time chief executive officer rather than the member of the Exchange who until that time had served in this largely honorary position for a two-year period.

The Big Board, which had requested the Martin Report and had publicized its findings, could not very easily turn down the recommendations, and so the reorganization was approved despite many misgivings from floor members about their reduced representation. Immediately afterward, a search was undertaken for a person to fill the new chairmanship, since Robert W. Haack—who until then had held the top staff post as president—did not wish to continue working for the Exchange.

Approximately ten men were contacted, either formally or informally, by the Big Board's selection committee before Needham was selected. Among them were Martin himself, who was asked to return to the organization that launched his illustrious career; Donald C. Cook of the American Electric Power Co., who once before had been considered; William Casey, a former chairman of the Securities and Exchange Commission; and John C. Whitehead, a partner of Goldman, Sachs & Co., the big investment banking house.

Needham was well aware that he was not the first choice of the selection committee, but to him the Exchange chairmanship was what can only be termed an ideal position for an ambitious and aggressive executive. At the age of forty-five he had already come a long way from his first job as a part-time messenger for the Continental Bank and Trust Company while he was still in school. Nevertheless, the opportunity for the chairman's post and the $300,000-plus salary that went with it was so overwhelming that he could hardly refuse the offer.

Already Needham had achieved success far beyond his dreams as a student at St. John's University, from which he graduated in 1951. A certified public accountant, he had been the New York partner of a Greensboro, North Carolina, accounting firm when President Nixon appointed him a member of the Securities and Exchange Commission in 1969. With this springboard to national prominence, he was in a key regulatory post and anxious to leave a Watergate-tinged Washington when the selection committee was searching for a Big Board chairman. After just three days of discussion, he was hired in 1972 and signed a five-and-a-half-year contract.

"I always viewed the job as a day-to-day proposition right from the start," Needham noted after he resigned in May 1976. "I couldn't say that at the time or I would have lost my credibility. But the nature of that job made too many decisions unpopular among a membership of such diverse interests, and I knew I wouldn't stay beyond five and a half years."

In fact, Needham's tenure lasted less than four years, during which the Exchange and the entire securities industry went through a period of enormous change. Congress and the SEC continued to demand action in the movement toward a national market system; negotiated commission rates for all orders from public customers to their brokers and from brokers to floor specialists were imposed by government fiat; and greater automation of floor facilities was pressed by the upstairs firms. The conflicts between the floor members and the upstairs members grew in intensity and often burst out into the open at the monthly meetings of the board of directors.

For example, there was a squabble early in Needham's reign at the Big Board regarding whether or not members would have to continue to be either partners or officers of their firms. The upstairs firms had long been resentful of this requirement—arguing that they should have the right to make this decision on the basis of individual merit—but the floor insisted that its prestige would suffer if the rule was abolished. The floor's view prevailed, and one of the floor directors exulted at the time, "Boy, we've got control again."

"We were always tipping and toeing and trying to stay in the middle," said Lee Vance, who had been a vice-president of the Exchange and executive assistant to Needham during his chairmanship. "But it was no good— the floor and the upstairs firms are just incompatible. So there were some strong outbursts around the board table."

Vance recalled one board meeting at which a heated argument developed between directors representing the floor and those representing the upstairs members. Bernard J. Lasker, a leading specialist and arbitrageur and then a member of the board, was in the thick of the discussion. "Bunny [Lasker's nickname] banged his first on the table and said he could call a meeting in a hotel room uptown and five hundred floor members would show up," Vance said. "He told the board that they should know who they were dealing with."

Needham tried to maneuver through the shoals and keep the Exchange afloat despite this dichotomy. He was on the telephone as often as three times a day with Donald T. Regan, chairman of Merrill Lynch, Pierce, Fenner & Smith and for a time vice-chairman of the Exchange, to work out strategy and tactics. He created a raft of committees to allow for greater participation in decision-making by those members who wanted to be active. He worked with specialists and floor brokers to develop the type of automated equipment with which they would feel comfortable. "I did everything I could for the floor, but it wasn't enough," Needham said.

What's more, there were times when he believed that the directors representing the floor were less than honest in their dealings with him. "I made a last-ditch fight in Washington," he said, "for fixed [nonnegotiated] floor brokerage [rates], and then I found out that rates really weren't fixed on the floor. There were all sorts of arrangements going on, but none of the three floor directors would disclose the actual practices."

In another instance, Needham felt that the board's decision to oppose the securities reform legislation in 1974, made at a meeting when the subject wasn't even on the agenda, was a serious error that forced him, as chief executive of the Exchange, to lobby in Congress for a position with which he had previously publicly disagreed. Long afterward, when he talked about the period during which he wound up antagonizing some of the key legislators pushing for securities reform, the pain and embarrassment that he suffered during his visits to Capitol Hill were obviously still a bad memory.

"I allowed myself to be in a position to do something I didn't believe in," he said. "I didn't like myself for having done it. I could have told the board to form a committee and given them the responsibility for stopping the legislation."

The Big Board was successful in blocking the legislation in 1974, but took no action as Congress returned the following year to pass the Securities Acts Amendments of 1975. These amendments have proven to be the most far-reaching securities legislation since the New Deal laws regulating the industry were passed in 1933 and 1934.

While Needham was becoming disenchanted with the

floor, the floor was becoming disenchanted with what they considered to be Needham's intransigence. To many floor members, he was too busy running around the country—and the world, for that matter—building up his image as a spokesman for the securities industry, instead of staying in his office and managing the Exchange. Some felt that he was too inaccessible, and resented the fact that a uniformed guard was at the head of the corridor leading to his spacious sixth-floor office at the Exchange building to screen out visitors. One veteran specialist bemoaned the idea that Needham and his three top staff officers were all accountants and therefore had a narrow view of the entrepreneurial activities that took place on the floor.

It was, however, Needham's pugnaciousness, an attribute that was frequently helpful to him in his role as national spokesman for American capitalism, that was resented by many floor members. In 1974, when the Exchange was fighting the Securities and Exchange Commission attempt to force negotiated commission rates on brokers for all transactions with their customers, Needham exclaimed, "You can tell the SEC that Needham said if we don't get what we want, we'll see them on the steps of Foley Square [the federal courthouse in New York]." Yet before long the Exchange decided not to battle the SEC on this score and went along with negotiated commissions.

Needham's *bête noire* turned out to be a specialist by the name of John J. Phelan, Jr., who was elected a director of the Exchange in 1974. The following year, when Regan resigned as vice-chairman, Needham—probably to his eternal regret—recommended that Phelan, as a representative of the floor, be elected to that post, and the board went along with his recommendation. Needham and Phelan were soon at swords' points, and before long, Needham was thinking of resigning.

"In the spring of 1975, I decided it was time to get out," he later asserted. "I had done the job they'd essentially hired me for and I was tired. I talked to several directors about this, including John Phelan."

For his part, Phelan, who joined his father's specialist firm in 1957 and started to become active in Exchange activities about a decade later, apparently would not have been unhappy to see Needham depart. "One of the great failures of the Exchange is its inability to articulate," he said one day as Needham's tenure in office was drawing to an end. "It really is a classic failure in marketing, for the more the Exchange comes under attack, the more it pulls in. All of life is a marketing process, and those that choose to ignore it are putting themselves on the road to extinction."

Although Needham took no further action regarding his resignation at that time, resentment against him—possibly more as a symbol of the reorganization and the floor's reduced role than as an individual—continued to build. A separate organization of floor members, called the Association for the Preservation of the Auction Market (APAM), was formed to lobby at the Exchange for more power to the floor, and it soon developed enough strength to petition for a change in the constitution that would add four directors, including two from the floor, to the board. Against the urgings of the board of directors, the full membership voted for this proposal and it was sent to the SEC for authorization. "Once a few specialists got up this petition, floor brokers would either sign it or they'd be dead," said Vance. "Otherwise no specialist would recognize them to get their tickets [buy and sell orders] in."

By November 1975 disillusionment with Needham from floor members was great enough for a group of directors to make an informal approach to William M. Batten, the recently retired chairman of the J. C. Penney Company and a fellow director, to find out whether he would be interested in the chairmanship. Batten, who was then chairman of a board committee studying the allocation procedure of Exchange-traded stocks to specialists, declined these overtures and told Needham about them. Nevertheless, the disillusionment grew.

As Needham later reflected on his final year in office, "A partnership breaks up intellectually and emotionally long before it breaks up legally. That's what happened here."

In January 1976 the Batten Report was delivered to the board, criticizing the lack of competition in awarding newly traded securities to just a single specialist on the floor and the failure of the Exchange to reallocate stocks when the specialists handling them showed themselves to be inadequate. Although the report was harsh on the floor, the floor, in turn, did not react adversely against Batten; on the contrary, it became even more impressed with his ability to grasp a complex subject in which he had little previous background and experience.

By the spring of that year the floor directors had grown so angry with Needham that they again approached Batten to take on the position, this time insisting that he do it as a public duty. At the age of sixty-six, Batten had worked long enough and was wealthy enough to decline such a demanding position in the limelight. But as a man who relished work as others relish leisure, he was anxious to get back into the saddle again and agreed to accept the post. He also managed, not so incidentally, to get a five-year contract, a salary that exceeded Needham's, and an agreement from APAM to drop its plan to increase the number of directors on the board.

After some secret meetings of groups of directors away from the halls of the Exchange, enough votes were lined up in April to ask for Needham's resignation. Phelan called him in Germany, where, as president of the International Federation of Stock Exchanges, he had been on a tour of European securities exchanges. Asked to come home immediately for an emergency board meeting, Needham knew that it was all over. He quit in May 1976, although he was paid for the full term of his contract, which ended in February 1978. In addition, he received a lifetime consulting contract to the Exchange which placed few limits on his right to take other positions.

In retrospect, Needham realized that his inability or unwillingness to go along with the demands of the floor members, many of which he regarded as wrong, was the major reason for his departure from the Exchange under such strained circumstances. "The floor is really a village," he said, "and floor people feel that the system pivots around them. They grow up with one another, they have intense likes and dislikes, and if someone does something they don't approve of, he can be ostracized.

"You know, this place is in many respects like a golf club. The floor people feel they own this place and they complain to the chairman if the toast isn't right in the luncheon club or there are no towels in the men's room. But I don't have any bad feelings toward these people. I just spent too much time in this job."

12

WILLIAM M. BATTEN:
A RETAILER
TAKES OVER

When William M. Batten was elected chairman and chief executive officer of the New York Stock Exchange in May 1976, there was general euphoria among the membership. Walter Frank, the veteran specialist, was delighted to welcome him because "he has no particular ax to grind." And one of the two vice-chairmen of the Exchange, Robert M. Gardiner, then chairman of Reynolds Securities, Inc., rhapsodized that Batten "is going to lead us all to the promised land."

This euphoria was based not only on anticipation of what Batten could achieve, but also on disillusion over what Needham had and had not done. Batten was hailed as the savior in the Exchange's time of trouble and as an elder statesman of business who would return the Big Board to it past days of glory.

The days of wine and roses did not last forever for Batten, as he quickly became enmeshed in the day-to-day problems of the Exchange: the battles with the Washington regulators and legislators, the conflicts between the floor and the upstairs members, and the shrinking base of brokerage firms and individual investors who use the Big Board's facilities. Nevertheless, the initial years of his term of office were crucial in determining the role of the New York Stock Exchange in the congressionally mandated national market system for trading securities—and Batten succeeded in shaping this role along lines in many respects suitable to his membership.

At first consideration, Batten was an unlikely candidate to be tapped to run the Big Board, the most discernible symbol of capitalism in the world's richest bastion of capitalism. At the time of his election he was a sixty-six-year-old retired retail executive who maintained his business ties by serving on a number of corporate boards as well as on the board of directors of the New York exchange since it was reorganized in 1972.

But a funny thing happened to the six-foot, balding executive on the way to his retirement—the Exchange found that it needed a new chairman and Batten found that he hated being away from full-time business life. On the first score, the directors and James J. Needham had for some time been coming to a parting of the ways. Needham had been growing increasingly disappointed with his lack of support from the power structure on the floor, while the resentment against his operating methods became greater and greater. In 1975 both were looking for and talking about ways to end their relationship, and by early 1976 it was only a matter of time before Needham's resignation was either asked for or voluntarily tendered.

During this same period, Batten was coming to the realization that he felt best when he was in harness. "I am not a golfer, I get bored when I go fishing, and I guess that since I've worked all my life, I have always had a lot of fun working," he said. "If I could think of more ways to have fun than working, I would stop working and do that."

For Batten, his lifetime's work had been at the J. C. Penney Company, the giant general-merchandise chain where he spent thirty-nine years. The West Virginia native and Ohio State University graduate joined Penney on a full-time basis as a salesman in 1935 and rose to the top of the ladder as chief executive officer in 1958. By the time he retired in 1974 as chairman and chief executive, he had earned a national reputation as an astute businessman and keen merchant who pushed Penney's annual sales to almost $7 billion, its profits to more than $119 million, and its number of stores to over two thousand.

In the course of his career at Penney, Batten's most meaningful accomplishment was the preparation of a report that the then vice-president wrote in 1957 on the character and policies of the company. In this report he developed the thesis that the corporation had failed to provide enough dimension for growth and suggested that a total distribution concept for both soft goods and hard goods was necessary for it to prosper in the years ahead. By anticipating the decline of the type of small soft-goods stores that Penney had principally been operating and by encouraging the opening of large department and junior department stores with all lines of merchandise, he helped to put Penney in a position of retailing leadership. And by showing his associates how to undertake this necessary revamping of the company, Batten positioned himself on the fast track that earned him the top spot at the chain-store concern, a spot that he held for sixteen years.

At his retirement, Batten was feted and toasted by his associates and friends. Walter B. Wriston, the chairman of Citicorp and Citibank, called him "wiser than a treeful of owls" and "the outstanding businessman in the country today." Others paid him similarly effusive tribute. But afterward came the reality of life—and Batten discovered that trips to his winter home on John's Island, Florida, and outside directorships on the boards of such companies as the American Telephone & Telegraph Corporation and the Boeing Company were not sufficient to fill his time.

As a result, he threw himself into his work as a public, or non–Wall Street, director of the Exchange. Late in 1974 Batten was named to the chairmanship of a committee of directors with the formal name of Committee to Study the Stock Allocation System. And during the fifteen months that he spearheaded this group he effectively broadened its mandate to include a redefinition of what the Exchange should be in the future.

He came to believe then, and believes more strongly than ever now, that the Big Board is basically a marketplace and will live or die based on that function alone. Its other functions as a trade association and a self-regulatory organization are secondary, according to the Batten viewpoint, to the inherent worth of the Exchange as an auction market providing an effective meeting place for buyers and sellers of securities.

Within this overview, the Batten Committee, in January 1976, reached the conclusion—eventually winning the support of the entire board and the very specialists whose livelihoods might be affected by any change—that the allocation and reallocation of stock to specialists should be based primarily on performance. As an outsider with no vested interest either in change for the sake of change or in the status quo, Batten was able to make a persuasive presentation of what was then a radical departure from past practice.

The depth and thoughtfulness of what came to be known as the Batten Report convinced many directors, both on and off the floor, that Batten was the man to take over the chairmanship. Although he first demurred, Batten later accepted and negotiated a five-year, $2 million contract with a salary escalating yearly. And then he happily returned to the routine he knew as a retailer of long workdays; breakfast, luncheon, and dinner meetings; and heavy travel throughout the country.

"There are some people who say that unless you've grown up in a business, there's no way you can manage it," he noted. "I don't agree with that. The common denominator is managing people, and the techniques are the same whether it's the 1,500 people we have here or the 200,000 people we had at Penney's."

And while the slow-talking, fast-thinking Batten has had a lot to learn about the securities business in his position at the pinnacle, he did not have much to learn about management. "I'm not very good at shooting from the hip, nor do I like it very much," he admitted. "My style is to take the time to walk around a situation and retain the options for a decision until we have to make one."

By periodically walking around the floor, calling and meeting with officials of upstairs firms, and generally making himself available to the membership, Batten has given Wall Street the opportunity to make its own judgments of this outsider. In general, his marks have been good.

"It's the first time that the Exchange has had the benefit of corporate-type planning and corporate-type contingencies," said George Rose, senior floor partner of Lazard Frères & Co. "I think having a chairman with a merchandising background is very helpful," added Harry A. Jacobs, Jr., chairman of Bache Halsey Stuart Shields. And Robert W. Swinarton, vice-chairman of Dean Witter

Reynolds, lauded Batten's "credibility with corporate America."

But there have also been plenty of critics of Batten on and around the Exchange floor. For example, Harry M. Jacobson, a partner in the specialist firm of Adler, Coleman & Co., once said that "to those of us used to moving very quickly, it seems that he moves slowly." Lee Vance, who had been Needham's executive assistant, was even more blunt. "I'm personally convinced," he said, "that this guy could give Machiavelli lessons."

In Batten's reign, the problems, or what the optimists at the Exchange refer to as challenges, have been different from what they were when Funston or Haack or Needham was at the helm. His major consideration has been determining the New York Stock Exchange's place in the emerging national market system and ensuring that stock exchanges, particularly his exchange, play a major part in this new era. In some cases, his technique has been one of encouraging delay in federal actions that would dampen or negate the role of the Big Board until the national market system is fully operational.

For example, there were the years of dispute over the Exchange's Rule 390—its regulation that prevents members from certain types of trading elsewhere without first bringing bids and offers to the floor. The SEC had long ago concluded that this rule, and similar ones at other exchanges, were barriers to free and equal competition and should be removed. It chipped away at parts of the rule until just two restrictions remained: those forbidding members from acting as dealers off the Exchange in trades with their customers and forbidding members from acting as brokers off-board on both sides of a transaction.

When the commission tentatively decided in June 1977 that these final restrictions should be eliminated by January 1978, Batten sprung into action. He was the first person to testify at the SEC's hearings on the matter and afterward sent a detailed brief expanding on his views. He also mobilized support from the corporate community through personal letters to every chief executive officer of a company listed on the Big Board and speeches to businessmen in several major cities. As a result, the SEC backed off from its original target date and gave the Exchange more time to come up with new systems before abolishing one that had proved to be effective for many years.

Another change in the Batten era was the adoption of rules providing greater access to the Exchange's facilities. When a committee of directors proposed in late 1976 to widen access by creating new classes of membership in addition to the 1,366 permanent seats that traditionally existed, most of the floor members rose up in opposition. They fought vigorously against this proposal, attacked its proponents at meetings, and screamed to all who would listen that such a move would dissipate the value of their memberships while serving no constructive purpose.

Batten led the forces that worked to disarm the opposition to the access proposal. He warned them that the SEC was demanding that the Exchange be opened to more competition. He told them that more members could bring more orders to the Exchange and thereby benefit the entire Exchange community. And he pushed through ramifications of the original proposal in order to make them more palatable to the floor. So when the actual vote was finally taken in 1977, approval was granted to permitting the sale of two categories of annual memberships and allowing a member to "rent" his seat to another. Since then, there has been some backtracking by the members, although the final word from the SEC is not yet in.

The access crisis was a situation similar to many others that Batten had to confront soon after arriving at the Big Board, whereby the interests of the floor differed from the interests of the upstairs members. As in most of these cases, the upstairs firms saw themselves as providing the order flow without which there would be no raison d'être for the Exchange to exist. Becoming bolder with each passing year, these firms, led by senior partners or officers with considerable clout in the financial community, began making more and more demands for a greater voice in the Exchange management—even to the extent of asking for a vote in proportion to their order flow, rather than in proportion to their memberships.

To the floor, such views were anathema—and the veteran floor partners and officials, a clique involved in all major Exchange decisions, lost no time in letting Batten know how they felt. To them, the floor is the Exchange and its power should be increased rather than reduced. Batten was forced to spend many hours and days reconciling these conflicting opinions on how the Exchange should be organized and, at least at the start of his chairmanship, wound up walking a tightrope between them.

The early Batten years were also a period of contraction among member firms doing business with the public and among individuals with an interest in the stock market. As fears grew of new government regulations that would emphasize the importance of the dealer, or over-the-counter, securities markets at the expense of the Exchange auction markets, medium-sized and even large firms worried whether they had sufficient capital to do business in this new environment. A merger mania hit Wall Street, beginning in 1976, as some of the best-known brokerage and investment banking firms disappeared or became hyphenated partners with others.

At the same time, the number of stockholders in corporations was also falling. Shortly before Batten was installed as chairman, the Exchange released a study showing that the country's shareowner population fell 18 percent, to 25.2 million, in the five-and-a-half-year period ended in 1975. In addition, the median age of the average stockholder rose from forty-eight to fifty-three, indicating that younger people were significantly less attuned to Wall Street than their parents.

Characteristically, Batten set out to do something about this trend. "While it is important to learn from the events and mistakes of the past, it is unproductive to dwell on them," he said. And he launched a substantive marketing effort beginning with an attitudinal survey of stockholders and potential stockholders in order to try to come up with new ways of reaching—and, it was hoped, selling to—this audience with whatever services the Big Board could devise.

For even before Batten became chairman of the Exchange, he determined that the Big Board was a business and had to be managed like one. One of his first internal efforts was the establishment of an organization plan, filled with the kind of objectives, strategies, and projects dear to the hearts of corporate planners but foreign to the freethinkers on the floor. "We want to be the highest-quality, most cost-effective marketplace in the securities industry," Batten said. "And we can't sit with a pat hand."

Thus Batten has moved forward to modernize outdated methodology, streamline moldering traditions, and eliminate deadwood. Just as the debris on the floor is cleaned up at the end of each trading day, so has he placed a particular emphasis on cleaning up the residue of backwardness and negative thinking that still remains on the floor and elsewhere in the massive building that houses the Big Board.

"I love the retail business and that's why I like the floor of the Exchange," Batten said. "It's like a store at Christmastime."

PART IV

The
Floor in Action

13

For two decades from about 1940 to 1960, the power structure on the floor of the New York Stock Exchange was headed by two veteran specialists, Robert L. Stott and John A. Coleman. Their two firms—Wagner, Stott & Co. and Adler, Coleman & Co.—were, and still are, among the best-known and best-capitalized specialist units on the Big Board and handle some of its most widely traded stocks. And during their heyday, Stott and Coleman were forces to be reckoned with when it came to decisions being made by or imposed upon the Exchange.

In subsequent years, other specialists assumed the official and unofficial mantle of leadership over the floor community and, with it, the role of spokesman for the floor in dealings both within the Exchange and outside its walls. Bernard J. Lasker of Lasker, Stone & Stern was one who held sway in the mid to late 1960s, while John J. Phelan, Jr., of Phelan, Silver, Vesce, Barry & Co. acquired this power in the mid to late 1970s.

But it was Stott and Coleman who sat in the catbird seats when there were relatively few with the ability, perseverance, and courage to challenge them. The two men— close friends yet sometimes antagonists over issues at board of governors meetings—were each strong, assertive, and devoted to the New York exchange. And during their period of power, the Exchange achieved some of its finest days of glory.

Stott—who was first elected as a governor in 1935 when he was proposed by Richard Whitney—served on the policy-making board for a total of twenty years. During two of these years, 1941 to 1943, he was the chairman of the board and virtually unquestioned as the man truly in charge of the Exchange. During his chairmanship the Big Board was reorganized to cope with the changes brought about by the entry of the United States into World War II and the resignation of its first full-time president in many decades, William McChesney Martin. And for Stott it was a period in which the floor was unquestionably the epitome of Wall Street's financial strength.

"That's when the senior members of the commission houses were actually on the floor," he later recalled. "They were the brokers who executed the orders. There is no comparison today. Now there's a lot of people who can't make a decision and have to go back to ask somebody upstairs."

Reaching the peak of power at the New York exchange and dealing with these senior members of the commission houses was quite an accomplishment for Stott, a poor boy from Brooklyn who came to Wall Street as a clerk at the age of eighteen in 1918. Within five years this man who went to work instead of to college became a member of the New York Curb Exchange, the predecessor of the American Stock Exchange, when its trading was still done on the street.

In 1925 he co-founded, with his friend Leonard Wagner, the Wagner, Stott partnership, which developed over the next fifty years into one of the largest specialist units on the Big Board, with assets of some $37 million and annual turnover of 300 million shares. But it was not always so. Stott's early days on the Curb Exchange, when he and Wagner specialized in the stock of Electric Bond and Share Corporation, were hectic, tense, and ulcer-filled, day in and day out.

"There was so much volume that we used to work to one, two o'clock every morning just to get all the accounts squared away and everything cleared out for the next day," he said. In 1929, when the two partners decided to give up the specialist's book in Electric Bond and Share, the stock was split among five specialists—one for each day of the week—because no one else could handle the full trading activity.

Stott was married in 1928, and the couple took a be-lated honeymoon cruise to Bermuda the following year. When Stott returned to New York, the crash of October 1929 had already occurred, but he nevertheless decided to remain on Wall Street. On the day after Christmas he purchased a seat on the New York Stock Exchange and was followed there a week later by his partner, Wagner.

Among the major corporations that Wagner, Stott served as specialist were Gulf Oil, Union Carbide, National Steel, and Xerox. When the Chase Manhattan Bank became the first major bank listed on the New York exchange, Stott was assigned as the specialist in that key issue. "A lot of people think this job is as easy as shooting fish in a barrel," he said. "What we do daily would make some guys' hair stand on end."

The Wagner-Stott combination was successful because Stott's daring and willingness to gamble were comple-mented by Wagner's hesitancy and conservatism. As the firm prospered and the number of stocks Stott handled at

Post 16 increased, he broadened his outlook to include a deeper interest in Exchange activities. Membership on the board at age thirty-five was the first step of his climb to power. He was an active participant in the governors' deliberations during the late 1930s as the depression was coming to an end, and he stood out as the best candidate for chairman when the Exchange's governing body was split into two factions in 1941.

On the one hand was the Old Guard, the patricians on the floor from socially prominent families who still remained from the Richard Whitney era, even though Whitney himself had been disgraced and sent to jail for grand larceny. This group of board members, like many of their predecessors, wore the old-school tie, spent as many hours away from Wall Street as on it, and wanted to keep things as they were without interference from either the membership or the Securities and Exchange Commission.

On the other hand were the Young Turks, the men in their thirties and forties without such pedigrees who demanded changes in the way the Exchange should be managed. The influence of these brokers, while not as extensive as that of the Old Guard, had been slowly growing during the late 1930s, as their receptivity to ideas emanating from outside the boardroom created conflicts with the heretofore established way of governing the Big Board.

Stott stepped in to bridge this gap and, along with Emil Schram, the incoming president of the Exchange, brought a new order to the floor. The New York Stock Exchange of that day was still a very private institution in which the specialists were the kingpins, but it became more responsive to the greater input from other floor members and the Washington regulators. "It is entirely proper," Stott told the membership, "for you to give the management of the Exchange the benefit of your views and suggestions at any time or to criticize and find fault if you wish." During his two-year tour of duty, Stott was kept busy in the chairman's office from 7 A.M. to 7:30 P.M. daily devising new policies and procedures, but nevertheless continued to play a role as a partner on the floor for Wagner, Stott.

"As far as the public is concerned, we had a better market in those days," he said recently, with perhaps a slight trace of bias. "You could deal very quickly in large volume. You had a real auction market. When you held yourself out as a specialist, you had to be in a position to deal."

In his professional activities, Stott was in the vanguard of new developments at the Exchange, both during and after his chairmanship. He was the first specialist to hold large, institutional-size inventories of stocks so as to be better able to trade with his customers. He also handled the largest big-block trade of his era, when he was the specialist for a 100,000-share-plus order for Union Carbide common stock. He was an originator in his business, a conciliator in the boardroom, and a principal figure in operating the New York Stock Exchange during some of the most crucial years of its history.

Overlapping Bob Stott's period of power at the Big Board was the reign at the top of John Coleman. Born in 1901, one year after Stott, Coleman followed a similar path economically from the lower middle class to the upper class by his ability to trade securities on the floor. And in Exchange politics, Coleman became another mover and shaker in the 1940s and 1950s.

In addition, Coleman became even better known over the years as a leading Catholic layman and philanthropist who served as the financial confidant to New York archbishops Cardinal Francis Spellman and Cardinal Terence Cooke. By the age of nineteen he was already a member of the Cardinal's Committee of the Laity soliciting special gifts, and by the end of his career he was a Knight of the Order of Malta and a Papal Chamberlain.

These honors were a far cry from Coleman's origins as one of six children of a New York City policeman growing up on the West Side of Manhattan. At the age of fourteen —when he weighed 134 pounds and stood five feet, ten inches tall—he quit school to go to work and found a menial job on the floor of the New York exchange. "You might say it all began for me on June 22, 1916," he told an interviewer. "That was the day I went to work as a page. There was no tube system to deliver messages in those days, so we never stopped running."

In 1922 Coleman became a member of the Curb Exchange and two years later bought a seat on the Big Board—at that time the youngest person ever to join its ranks. In 1928 he and Paul Adler formed the specialist firm of Adler, Coleman, which now trades in such prestigious stocks as W. R. Grace & Co., the J. C. Penney Company, and the Squibb Corporation. Coleman kept the badge number 13 that he wore as a page when he became a specialist (it did not signify bad luck for him!), and to this day that badge is worn by a partner in the Adler, Coleman firm.

Coleman prospered as a trader—"John Coleman doesn't trade to lose money," said one envious competitor—by following his own advice to "always buy the best stocks." Before long he sought out other activities within the Exchange structure. He began working on committees, where he was noticed by the hierarchy, and was first elected a governor in 1938. He also served on the Conway Committee, which had recently been established by the board to determine how to reorganize the Exchange into an organization with a paid president and full administrative staff. When Stott was named chairman of the Exchange in 1941, Coleman was elected vice-chairman, and in 1943 Coleman became chairman in his own right.

During the years of his chairmanship, Coleman helped to keep the Exchange functioning in a period of dull trading days due to the exigencies of World War II. He also developed a reputation as a tough, hard-nosed administrator who would brook no nonsense after he had made a decision. Coleman made many friends, but he also made many enemies—floor members and others who were angered by his autocratic ways while holding the power of the Big Board in his hands. Yet despite all of his days of wealth and power, he remained to the end of his life as wide-eyed and enthusiastic about the floor of the New York Stock Exchange as he was when a newcomer to the Wall Street scene.

"This is the greatest business in the world," he once remarked, "because it's all built on trust. You don't have any contracts. It's just word of mouth—character. We do it without witnesses or this or that, and to my knowledge nobody has ever reneged on a contract made on the floor. Fascinating, I enjoy every minute."

In the 1960s the mantle of floor leadership passed in fact and in name to Bernard ("call me Bunny") Lasker. Assuming power at a time when the Exchange was buffeted by the specter of failing member firms that threatened to create panic on Wall Street, Lasker helped to bring order out of chaos and to restore a measure of stability after one of the sharpest market declines in history.

"The firms that have the talent to adjust to almost any circumstance are going to live," he said time and again. "You've just got to be able to take advantage of the breaks when they come."

Lasker himself, throughout his business career, knew how to take advantage of breaks. Born in New York in 1910, he was raised on the West Side of Manhattan in a comfortable family until his father, an importer of sponges, died in 1924. College was out of the question, so Lasker got a job in 1927 as a runner for a brokerage firm called Hirsch, Lilienthal & Co. From that entry-level position he followed the self-made-man pattern of moving upward to fame and fortune.

Lasker bought a seat on the New York exchange in 1939 and eight years later formed a partnership with Edwin H. Stern, Jr., that continued for more than twenty years until Stern died. Their company, now known as Lasker, Stone & Stern, is a specialist firm that trades with commission brokers and also does a large arbitrage business. Lasker is an arbitrageur—a professional trader who takes advantage of temporary price differences in related securities by such techniques as buying securities expected to be valued higher in the future because a potential acquirer may offer a premium over the market price— par excellence.

By the time Lasker was first elected to the Exchange board of governors in 1965, he was a millionaire and willing and able to become deeply involved in Exchange politics. Already considered a key voice representing the floor constituency, he solidified his position by vociferously defending the floor, and the entire Exchange, from opposition in Washington, Wall Street, or anywhere else. By 1967 he was the natural choice for vice-chairman when Gustave L. Levy was elected chairman, and two years later Lasker succeeded to the chairmanship.

A tall, imposing, affable man, Lasker is a Republican and a conservative whose era in power culminated during the administration of President Richard M. Nixon. As the go-go decade on Wall Street, when the stock market pushed toward record levels, came to an end in 1970 with a tremendous drop in prices, Lasker proved to be the right man in the right place at the right time. His friendship with Nixon of more than ten years—a friendship built on mutual interests and Lasker's fund-raising for Nixon's campaigns—enabled him to obtain White House action that year in an effort to stem the market collapse.

Because of Lasker's persistence in discussions with Nixon, the President scheduled a widely publicized dinner at the White House with Wall Street and business leaders in May 1970. The day after the announcement of the meeting, there was a thirty-two-point gain in the Dow Jones Industrial Average. The day after the dinner the Dow rose another twenty-one points, and before too long the market had been turned around from its disastrous course. The Nixon-Lasker dinner had served its purpose well.

Lasker's other major accomplishment as chairman was the establishment in 1970 of a surveillance committee—everyone on the floor called it "the crisis committee"—to oversee member firms' financial affairs. Lasker and Felix G. Rohatyn of Lazard Frères & Co. were the key participants on the committee, whose major task was to make sure that (1) individual investors did not lose funds and

(2) public confidence in the Exchange did not disappear because of the impending liquidation of some of the biggest brokerage houses on Wall Street. Before the committee finished its work, three giants of the industry had to be rescued by other firms: Hayden, Stone & Co., Goodbody & Co., and Francis I. DuPont & Co. But the Streetwide bloodbath that many people on and off the floor had predicted did not occur, and Lasker concluded his two-year term as chairman with the Exchange still functioning as a viable institution.

"There are thirty-five different things that can go wrong, and if I have one big loss, I'll be back where I started," Lasker said a few years after leaving the chairmanship—a post to which he had given such single-minded devotion during bleak years for the Exchange. But no one on the floor really thinks that Bunny Lasker can ever be kept away from the action that has been so much a part of his life for more than fifty years.

Today the single most powerful broker on the floor is a specialist and one of the two vice-chairmen of the Exchange—now the top post in the hierarchy held by someone who is not a paid member of the administration—by the name of John J. Phelan, Jr. Phelan, who headed the firm of Phelan & Silver, merged it with Vesce & Barry to change the name to Phelan, Silver, Vesce, Barry & Co. ("We were a vaudeville act and decided to be a law firm," he joked.) The stocks he handles include the Southern Company, International Harvester, and Control Data Corporation. And the stories of his power are legion.

It was Phelan who took the lead in deposing James J. Needham as chairman of the Exchange in 1976, after Needham had lost the confidence of the board of directors. It was Phelan who pushed for the development of an intermarket trading system (ITS) linking the New York exchange with the regional exchanges around the country in order to maintain the Big Board's leading edge under the congressionally mandated national market system. And it was Phelan who anticipated the displeasure of the floor membership with the exchange's posture vis-à-vis the outside world and demanded more concentration on marketing.

Phelan's entire being is currently thrown into the fight being waged by the Exchange to retain its dominant position as a trading mechanism. Spending almost as much time in his vice-chairman's office on the sixth floor of the Exchange building as he does on the floor, he is continually involved in administrative meetings and planning strategy for the days, months, and years ahead. "The Exchange has to adjust to the makeup in the mix of member firms," he asserted.

Phelan became a member of the Exchange in 1957 after joining his father's firm and was elected senior partner in 1966 upon the death of his father. Soon afterward he became an Exchange official—the first level of elected authority over the membership—and was named to the board in 1971. Phelan went off the board in 1972 when the Exchange was reorganized in accordance with the Martin Report, but returned in 1974. The following year he was named vice-chairman, a post he has held ever since.

"Today everybody wants to be a chief," he noted. "But we have to remember that most of the things that are a threat to the specialist system are a threat to the Exchange itself. No one can speak for the securities industry as a whole, because no one can understand the securities industry as a whole."

But if no one can speak for the securities industry, Phelan, as much as anyone else, can speak for the floor of the New York Stock Exchange. And like Stott, Coleman, and Lasker before him, his words—based on experience, knowledge, and the power to lead those around him—are listened to with respect by the majority of the brokers on the floor.

14

THE
OLD-TIMERS

In every generation on the floor of the New York Stock Exchange there are the Young Turks and the Old Guard. The Young Turks are usually in their thirties or forties and have been members long enough to feel that changes are overdue in the way the Exchange is run. The Old Guard is generally led by members in their fifties, sixties, or older who attempt to maintain the status quo that has brought them to power. What is sometimes overlooked in discussions of their conflicts, however, is that the Young Turks of one generation often become the Old Guard of the next.

Thus the old-timers at the Exchange today were once Young Turks in their own right who faced many of the same problems and frustrations that stymie younger members now. Their histories indicate how they have changed as the Exchange has changed, and their revelations point up many of the differences between the old and the new. Listen to their stories about the past and the flavor of their era comes through loud and clear.

George M. L. La Branche, Jr., joined the Big Board before October 29, 1929, the "Black Tuesday" that permanently changed the face of Wall Street, and is ranked sixth among all of its active members in terms of seniority. La Branche, at the age of seventy-seven, is still active on the floor, where he is the senior partner of the specialist firm of La Branche & Company. "I've been on the floor every day since 1923," he said—March 15, 1923, to be exact.

"My grandfather was a member and my father was a specialist," he noted, going on to repeat a theme that old-timers on the floor voice again and again. "In the old days, the heads of the commission firms were on the floor and most of the decisions were made on the floor. Today most of the decisions are made off the floor and transmitted to the floor, where they are executed."

But La Branche, who does not believe that all the changes have been bad, can, in retrospect, see some of the evils that existed on the floor during his early years on Wall Street. "A group of people used to gather together on the floor like a traders' union and would deal only with each other," he said. "Now we've got many more rules and regulations that govern our trading. Of course, rules and regulations do not create honesty. Honesty comes from within."

La Branche, who now runs a firm with eleven partners who are specialists in more than forty stocks, doesn't by any means think, though, that the Exchange is an easier place to work in 1979 than it was in 1929. "The economic, social, and political fabric of our entire lives has been changed," he observed. "But if you have a thin skin, you don't belong on the floor. And if you can't love the work you're doing, don't do it."

The white specialist's badge bearing the numbers 2297 belonged to Benjamin Einhorn, the senior partner of

Einhorn & Company, who became a member of the Exchange in 1929.

"I started as a page on the floor in 1925 when I was seventeen years old for fourteen dollars a week," he once said. "I came down here to make enough money to go to college at Rensselaer Poly, but I never got there. I went to NYU at night and never finished."

Like many of those who came up through the ranks at the Exchange without family connections or inherited wealth, Einhorn saw the floor as a great melting pot where success is obtainable regardless of origin. "I don't think there ever has been a place of such opportunity for people of such diverse backgrounds," he asserted. "I didn't take a lunch hour for thirty years because I was so busy. But we developed a tremendous loyalty to the Exchange, and we still have it."

Although Einhorn's loyalty to the Exchange was maintained for more than fifty years, his ability to recognize its failings, past and present, did not become blurred. "When I first came here in 1929," he said, "the specialist was doing you a favor by taking your order. Now there is an obligation to do so and a realization that we are a quasi-public institution. You receive the right to function in return for fulfilling certain duties."

When he stood in front of Post 2, Section G, as he did for decades, Einhorn fulfilled the two primary functions of a specialist in "making" a market in a security: buying and selling for his own account and acting as a broker's broker by handling limit orders left by other members until they can be executed. His clerks, in buff-colored jackets, were inside the trading post maintaining the long, narrow specialist books, while the floor reporters who transcribe all sales stood near him on the outside.

"Many people of my generation have retired or passed away," Einhorn noted toward the end of his career. "This business has always been a business of great tension. And our biggest problem today is uncertainty about the future." Ben Einhorn died in 1979.

Elmer M. Bloch, a specialist since 1929 and a member of the firm of H. L. Goldberg & Company, has one of the more unusual backgrounds at the New York Stock Exchange. His father, Dr. Julius Bloch, was rabbi of the Touro Synagogue, the famed national landmark in Newport, Rhode Island, and sixth in a line of rabbis in his family. While in college, Elmer Bloch supported himself as a violinist and leader of a dance band. And after graduation, he joined the R. H. Macy executive training squad with the intention of becoming a retailer.

Before too long, though, Bloch was fired by Macy's and wound up buying and selling stocks instead. He was first a runner; then a trainee; then, after obtaining a seat, a commission broker; and finally a specialist, in 1931. "I'll never forget in those days there was a guy with a prestigious firm of commission brokers who treated specialists like dirt," Bloch said. "Then he became a specialist himself and people on the floor called that the greatest conversion since Martin Luther."

Bloch, whose reputation on the floor for honest dealing is equaled by his reputation as a raconteur, still has great affection for the men whom he worked with during his early years on Wall Street. "Fellows went to any length to help you out in those days," he noted. Recalling one incident where a specialist who lost all of his money in the market was quickly able to borrow $250,000 from five members to get started again, he added, "Of course, the next day those guys were in the crowd trying to take that money away."

Yet along with this affection for his home away from home for more than five decades goes a sense of humor that prevents him from taking himself and the Exchange as an institution too seriously. "I remember my father's comment when he first came down here," Bloch said. "He said that it reminded him vaguely of the zoo."

The pattern of progress on the floor from runner to page to clerk to member has been repeated many times over. Another frequent pattern is the movement of members from commission broker or two-dollar broker to specialist, long considered the premier position on the floor. Such was the rise of Emil J. Roth, whose name is one of the two in that of his specialist firm, Hirshon, Roth & Company.

"My uncle Saul Ungerleider moved to New York from Cleveland in 1926 and started his own firm," he said. "I was a favorite nephew and he offered me an opportunity to come to Wall Street. I started as a runner, then I was a margin clerk, and then I marked the board. Before I was twenty-one I became a page on the floor and once had a ten-dollar gold piece handed to me by Richard Whitney."

Roth became a member in 1928 with his uncle's commission brokerage firm and stayed there until it merged into another—a firm that through many more mergers later became the nation's largest, Merrill Lynch, Pierce, Fenner & Smith—when he went out on his own as a floor trader. In 1950 he joined forces with Hirshon & Company to become a specialist.

"I noticed even as a youngster that the Stock Exchange authorities became more sophisticated each year in promulgating rules that worked to the benefit of the investing public," he observed. "I don't think that members take advantage of the public."

Although he certainly qualifies as an old-timer on the floor, Roth does not go along with the theory that prevails among many members that the actions of the Securities and Exchange Commission in recent years have all been detrimental to the Big Board. "Many things that the SEC have done have been for the stability of the business," he said. "The Stock Exchange only has control over its members. It requires a federal agency to be able to do the kind of policing that's good for the industry. I really believe that."

Henry M. Watts, Jr., is another Big Board veteran who recognized long ago that the specialist was the king of the floor. But he decided to carve out a niche for himself in floor brokerage and, in doing so, built the biggest such firm in executing for some three hundred other brokers, building a nationwide communications network with them and clearing all of the paper work connected with their transactions. As a result, he became as well known and played as important a role as any specialist of his era.

"I started as a two-dollar broker in March 1929, when I was twenty-five years old, and the crash came in October," Watts said. "It took me ten years to pick myself up."

Watts picked himself up by co-founding the firm of Mitchel, Schreiber, Watts & Company in 1938. He still serves as its chairman, although the concern was sold in 1978 to the Angeles Corporation, another securities company. His strong point has always been good, fast execution of orders, and his skill in that field has won him the plaudits of his peers—plaudits that culminated in his election to the chairmanship of the board of governors in

1962, a time when that post was still held by an active member.

"I'm on the floor myself three hours a day," he noted. "An individual two-dollar broker can do business cheaper than us, but we can do more. We don't have to clear through anyone, and we do a lot of work for the firms we do business with to keep them happy."

So what does Watts, a man who rose to the top doing it his way, think about the specialists on the floor of the New York exchange? "A good specialist can be very, very constructive," he responded. "Even if the man has a stripe of larceny in him, he now has to abide by the rules. In the old days, they used to drive us nuts and frequently slice up some poor young man new to the floor. It was really a dogfight. Now when we sometimes get complaints about specialists, we investigate them. If they weren't running orderly markets, we would tell them to change."

Watts admits, however, that he misses some of the color that used to be on the floor. "Once one member said to another, 'I'll match you for everything in your right hand pocket,' and the second guy lost. He thought he had $5 in his pocket, but he pulled out $1,800 and handed it to the other guy. You know, that's the basis of the Exchange—if you make a trade, you're good for it."

An active member of the Buttonwood Club, named for the tree under which the Exchange was founded and peopled by brokers who have been members for at least twenty years, Watts is also a booster of the Buttonwood Foundation, through which scholarships are awarded to children of Exchange employees. "I'm probably being an old bastard criticizing that things aren't what they used to be," he said. "But people then tended to be a lot more responsible. You can always tell a sheep from a goat."

Walter W. Stokes, Jr., who heads the specialist firm of Stokes, Hoyt & Company, is a third-generation Exchange member. His grandfather joined in 1878, his father joined in 1902, and he joined in 1929. Here's how he tells about his becoming a member of the Big Board:

"In 1925 I graduated from Yale and got married five days later with no visible means of support. I worked for six months at the Union National Bank of Schenectady, New York, when I left because there was no future there. I went into my father's office in 1926, and because he wanted to retire at fifty, he transferred his seat to me in 1929."

"Black Tuesday" arrived exactly five months after Stokes became a member of the Exchange, and the next few months were as hectic as he has ever seen. "I went to the john one day to take a pee and I mentioned to the guy next to me that I had three thousand shares of a stock to sell at the market," he said. "He told me that he had ten thousand shares of that stock to buy at the market. So we made a trade while peeing."

In those years there was a great sense of friendship among the members, and some of them later formed an informal organization called the Silly Bastards Club. "We were just a bunch of guys who had a drink before lunch and would talk about the stupid things that people did on the floor," Stokes recalled.

Stokes remembers the bitter moments over the years as well as the amusing ones. "Once I did a financial favor for a broker," he observed. "Two years later, he comes in with flowers for a competitive specialist in one of our stocks. I never forgave him for that."

That incident occurred during the 1930s, when competitive specialists were in vogue. Although the Exchange management has been trying recently to promote competitive specialists again in an effort to demonstrate to Washington legislators and regulators its competitive spirit, Stokes does not feel that this concept works. "It's death," he said. "[Commission] brokers wind up with two friends and two enemies. I don't see anything that can't be handled by one specialist."

Most of the floor old-timers have certain distinguishing characteristics in common: loyalty to the Exchange, a gambler's instinct, an ability to think and act quickly, an awareness of the importance of their function. Whether they become members of the Exchange as a wealthy son or son-in-law of a member or as a boy from the other side of the tracks promoted from a clerkship, they usually wind up with many of the same attitudes, economic biases, and political leanings by the end of their careers. For better or for worse, the melting pot at the corner of Broad and Wall streets still seems to work.

15

Every weekday at slightly before 9 A.M., Thomas M. Schwalenberg arrives at work on Wall Street. Dressed in a dark suit and dark tie, he goes to his 20 Exchange Place office at deCordova, Cooper & Co., a member firm of the New York Stock Exchange, where he checks the daily long and short positions—the amount of stock the firm owns and the amount it has sold short with the expectation of buying it back later at a lower price. Then, about 9:45, he leaves for the floor of the Big Board, where he will spend the next six hours buying and selling stock.

For Tommy Schwalenberg is a specialist—a brokers' broker and a direct beneficiary of the specialist system that began when James Boyd broke his leg in 1875—and one of the individuals at the New York exchange who are responsible for what is called "making a market" in the more than two thousand common and preferred stocks traded there. These specialists, who must possess great mental and physical agility to survive, actually run an auction for other brokers, assess the bids and offers brought to them, and help determine the price of the securities for which they are responsible. Limited by strict Exchange rules and guided by their own instincts regarding short-term price fluctuations, specialists like

Schwalenberg are responsible for maintaining orderly markets in their stocks and at the same time working to make a profit for themselves.

Schwalenberg, who is only thirty-four years old, has been a member of the Exchange for twelve years and has worked there for seventeen. Although, unlike many specialists, he had no family connections when he arrived on Wall Street, he has been quite successful both professionally and financially, and is now a partner of deCordova, Cooper. His salary is $42,000—far below the median for those engaging in this lucrative field—but he is still young, has the potential to earn a six-figure income before too long, and even now gets 8 percent of the firm's profits, in keeping with his percentage of the partnership. In short, Schwalenberg has achieved the good life on Wall Street.

"When I came down to Wall Street, I knew nothing about it," he said. "But I found it enjoyable and my mode of transportation to the future."

A native of Queens, one of the five boroughs of New York City, Schwalenberg had no intention of working on Wall Street as a boy. But while attending college he needed money to help pay his tuition and so in 1960 got a fifty-two-dollar-a-week job as a page on the Exchange floor. A page's job, one of the lowest in the Exchange hierarchy, involves taking messages and order confirmations from specialists' posts in the center of the floor to brokers' booths on the edges. Schwalenberg found the atmosphere on the floor to be electric and fascinating—and so he dropped out of college. From that moment on, Schwalenberg was committed to making a career for himself in the financial community.

"It was different than it is now," he remembered.

"There was a very strict code. Everyone had a haircut, and if you didn't have a haircut, you'd be out. If you didn't shave, you went home. Dungarees were out, too. There was no talking by pages, no reading, no running. What a difference!"

Schwalenberg ran with his messages—actually he walked extremely fast, since running is still forbidden by Exchange rules—while others merely sauntered, and he was soon noticed by many members. DeCordova, Cooper offered him a position as a clerk in 1962 at $110 a week and Schwalenberg gladly took it, since it represented a raise in both salary and status. As a specialist's clerk, Schwalenberg stood shoulder to shoulder with a dozen or so other clerks inside a trading post on the floor, keeping records for their bosses and listening intently in order to record every trade completed.

Schwalenberg again surpassed his colleagues by proving to be smarter, faster, and more accurate than anyone else and was soon promoted to chief clerk. In 1965, when one of the deCordova, Cooper partners retired, the firm followed an Exchange tradition by offering a partnership to its chief clerk. Schwalenberg was the chief clerk and thus at the age of twenty-two—just one year older than the minimum age for Exchange membership—became a member, a partner with a $12,000-a-year salary and a 2 percent share of the business.

The way Schwalenberg purchased his seat turned out to be different from the way most people in his position wind up as members of the Exchange. At first he did it traditionally, via what Wall Street calls an ABC agreement. This is an agreement signed by the member and the firm he works for, whereby the firm puts up the money even though the seat is listed (as it must be) in the member's name. If the member at a future time wishes to sell the seat, he must first purchase it from the firm or arrange for the firm to be compensated before he can transfer it to someone else.

In Schwalenberg's case, he obtained an ABC seat in 1965, but six years later, when his firm merged with another and was in the process of being reorganized, he had to acquire it on his own if he wanted to keep the membership. So, with the value of a membership then at $215,000, he paid $15,000 and signed a note to pay the remainder over a twenty-year period at $10,000 a year. With the movement in recent years toward a national market system in which the Exchange would be just one link, the value of Big Board seats has periodically declined from that amount—its all-time high was $515,000 in 1968 and 1969—and Schwalenberg at times owed more for his membership than it was actually worth. In 1978, for example, seat prices ranged from $105,000 to $46,000.

Schwalenberg doesn't dwell on the paper loss he may have at a given point on his Exchange seat because he realizes that his membership has been his ticket to a high-income career. Now his day is wrapped up in the tensions of the stock market, and he earns his living by anticipating and reacting to the pressures that this market brings every day to every member and employee on the floor.

The day begins at Post 10 where Schwalenberg and another dozen specialists stand in front of the horseshoe-shaped trading post to await the arrival of brokers, traders, and market makers who want to buy or sell the stocks they handle. Schwalenberg is responsible for the trading in two common stocks, British Petroleum and Tandycrafts, and sometimes assists one of his partners when the trading gets heavy in their stocks. The premier security at deCordova, Cooper is International Business Machines, which frequently requires the attention of two specialists, and Schwalenberg often pitches in there when the action increases in intensity. But it is for his own two stocks that he is always at the ready to keep up with every detail.

"I can't relive today what I did yesterday," he said. "I have to trade to make money today. If you're in the market professionally, you should be in and out all the time."

What Schwalenberg does, therefore, is to start each day anew. Whatever amount is in deCordova, Cooper's inventory of shares of British Petroleum and Tandycrafts is valued on a per-share basis according to the closing price the previous day. Schwalenberg's role is to make a trading profit on shares added to or subtracted from that inventory during the day.

For example, if Tandycrafts closed at, say, $25 on a Wednesday, Schwalenberg will work from that base and probably open the auction on Thursday at 24⅞ bid and 25⅛ offered. This means that he stands ready to buy all shares offered at $24.875 and to sell all shares needed at $25.125. If a time arrives when he does not own any Tandycrafts shares and a request comes in from a buyer, he will sell them "short." The market price of Tandycrafts will usually rise and fall by ⅛ of a point, or 12½ cents, many times during the day and Schwalenberg's task is to sell higher and buy lower than the next guy as often as possible.

But as a specialist, with what could be termed a monopoly situation as the market maker for specific stocks on the floor of the world's largest securities exchange,

Schwalenberg must also operate under certain restrictions imposed on all of its specialists by the Big Board. Not only does the Exchange periodically examine each specialist's books and records during surprise inspections and routinely ask the brokers on the floor to rate every specialist's performance, but it also requires that these specialists refrain from trading in certain situations until the public has an opportunity to do so. Thus when public limit orders are in a specialist's "book"—orders to buy or sell stock at a different level from the market price that are left with the specialist until they can be executed—they must take precedence over a specialist's own dealings. Similarly, when a broker in the "crowd" around a specialist's post wants to buy or sell an issue, he also gets first call over the specialist who has the same thing in mind.

Schwalenberg, like the other specialists, lives with this system because he knows that he can still operate flexibly enough to make a profit in his business. No one is closer to the trading in a particular stock, no one has a better feeling for the nuances of its movement than the specialist who handles it. And this closeness and feeling can be correlated into many dollars of profit for the alert specialist on the floor. "I don't like to lose money," Schwalenberg said. "Not ten cents."

For Schwalenberg and the other specialists on the New York exchange, the key tool through which they function is the order book—a loose-leaf binder about fourteen inches long and just four inches wide in which their limit orders are entered. Even in this era of computerization and advanced electronic technology, New York exchange specialists use the same kind of book that has been used for generations to maintain the records needed to operate from moment to moment. Its very simplicity and ease of entry makes it useful in the operation of the floor's auction market.

Thus in Schwalenberg's book for Tandycrafts a series of pages is maintained, with buy orders on the left side of the book and sell orders on the right. One page contains all of the limit orders at prices from 24 through 24⅜, with corresponding selling prices listed on the facing page. The next two pages will have space for the buy and sell orders at 24½ to 24⅞. Rules separate the price categories on a page and written entries are made by Schwalenberg when appropriate.

One day, for example, when Tandycrafts was selling for 24½, Schwalenberg may have put an entry of "4 EFH" under 24 on the buy page for 24 through 24⅜. It would mean that E. F. Hutton & Company, a big brokerage firm that deals with the public, wanted to purchase 400 shares of Tandycrafts for a customer when the price dropped to 24. At the same time, four different brokers may have had sell orders listed totaling 1,200 shares at 24. If and when the price were to drop to 24, Schwalenberg would arrange for the sale to Hutton of 400 shares of Tandycrafts from the broker or brokers on the sell side whose orders first came into the book, and would cross out the respective entries. Schwalenberg might buy all or part of the remaining shares himself, depending on market conditions. Before long, new limit orders would be brought to him at different prices by other brokers and the sequence would continue. By the end of the day, Schwalenberg would probably handle and execute limit orders for thousands of shares of Tandycrafts—most of which would show up on his book either as executed orders or as held over until the next day.

Schwalenberg, a trim, five-foot, ten-inch man who is an intense tennis player in his spare time, has his own special way of measuring the trend of the market beyond the standard tools (the half-hourly Dow Jones Industrial Average, the hourly New York Stock Exchange index, and so on) used by other specialists and brokers. He and his friends on the floor call it the "Schwally index," which is nothing more than a system for charting the net difference between the number of stocks advancing and the number declining at any given time. Schwalenberg lists this difference—easily obtainable through the computer display console behind him on his post—every fifteen minutes on the back of an unused stock report card and thus has a sensitive running tally of market direction.

"If there were nine hundred declines on balance at midday, I'd be cautious if an advancing trend started because it would probably be technical in nature and not long-lasting," he said. "When the market goes down with over five hundred issues, it's digging itself into a hole and I'd have to look at the rallies coming afterward very skeptically."

These esoterica are likely to mean little to the average person away from the floor, but they are of great importance to those whose lives and livelihoods are involved in this tightly knit financial community. For Wall Street is a place where many thousands of dollars can change hands when a stock goes up or down just one eighth of a point. And any trading edge over his fellow professionals that Schwalenberg gets by using his "Schwally index" can mean thousands of dollars to him and his firm every day. As one member looking at the trading results achieved by the use of this index remarked, "Gee, Tommy, you read palms."

For Schwalenberg, the youngest of the five partners at deCordova, Cooper, the floor and its lore represent his world, to which he has given a lifelong commitment. As he sees the changes that are enveloping the Big Board, diminishing somewhat its overwhelming position of supremacy in the industry and creating a vastly different securities trading mechanism, he recognizes that he and his fellow specialists may be taking on a new role, too. Yet Schwalenberg, who is in the eye of the hurricane that is created every day when buyers and sellers of securities come together at the foot of Broad and Wall, is supremely confident that his generation on the New York Stock Exchange floor will rise to tomorrow's challenges, just as his predecessors have done in the past.

"Many changes that are coming," he said, "are going to complicate our lives. But I have no doubt at all that I still could make a good living here."

16

The first women appeared on the floor of the New York Stock Exchange during World War II, when many of the men who worked there went off to the Army. But their appearance was temporary, since they were replaced when the war ended and the male employees returned. Furthermore, they were clerks and pages who worked for members rather than members themselves. Whoever heard of a woman member of the New York Stock Exchange?

Today that question seems ridiculous, since the women's movement and the federal government's drive toward equal opportunities for women have long since brought females into this former bastion of masculinity. Although the majority of the women on the floor are still clerks and pages—over the last decade these jobs have been opened to women with no restrictions—there are a few full-fledged women brokers among the hundreds of males who gather every day at 11 Wall Street to buy and sell stocks and bonds. And thereby hangs a tale of change in Wall Street that would have been scoffed at as recently as the early 1960s.

From its origins, the brokerage business has been male-oriented, with women traditionally relegated to secondary, or support, positions. The floor in particular, with its clublike atmosphere and ribald male humor, was off limits to women for generations. The entire atmosphere on the floor was one that it was felt would make women feel uncomfortable, whether trading was hectic and electricity was in the air or trading was slow and there was time for horseplay and pranks.

It wasn't until 1940, in fact, that the first female general partner was named at a New York Stock Exchange member firm. A small firm, Belden & Co., appointed Muriel Audrey Bailey to that position, and Wall Street wondered how a woman could handle the responsibilities. Miss Bailey did her job well, however, and led the way for other women partners and—when the Exchange permitted its member firms to organize as corporations as well as partnerships—officers of brokerage firms that belonged to the Big Board.

But women were not permitted to become members of the Exchange itself until one woman, Muriel F. Siebert, decided to test the written and unwritten rules barring such membership in 1967. By the time that Miss Siebert made her application for membership, she already had credentials as a well-respected and well-paid analyst of the stock market. Nevertheless she, too, encountered difficulties along the long road before achieving her goal of owning a seat on the Exchange and wearing a member's badge.

Miss Siebert, known in the financial community as Mickie, entered the securities business in 1954, with a major in economics and accounting but with no practical experience in investing. "I came to New York with five hundred dollars and a beat-up Studebaker," she recalled. "I didn't move up by following the pack."

Miss Siebert's first job was as a sixty-five-dollar-a-week research trainee for the firm then called Bache & Co. and now named Bache Halsey Stuart Shields. She was assigned to follow the aviation industry and built her career on the knowledge she accumulated about investment opportunities and the timing of purchases and sales of securities in that field. "The transportation analyst had railroads, shipping, and airlines," she said. "He decided the airlines didn't have much of a future, so he gave them to me. That put me in the right place when the aerospace and jet aviation booms started."

After a few years at Bache, she worked for Selig Altschul, an aviation consultant, and then for Utilities and Industries Management Corporation as an analyst and portfolio manager. "In 1958 I wrote to one hundred and fifty brokerage firms asking for a job and no one answered," she noted. "Then the New York Society of Security Analysts sent out my résumé with my initial instead of my first name."

Miss Siebert finally did land a job as a senior analyst with Shields & Co., now also part of Bache Halsey Stuart Shields. At the beginning her work consisted entirely of analysis, and she developed a following among institutions for the quality of her research. When one institutional investor who was especially pleased with a piece of research offered her an order as a token of thanks, she wasn't sure what to do. So she asked her boss, a partner in the firm, who barked at her, "Get out of here and get the order."

Learning quickly how to get orders, Miss Siebert became a star selling analyst—a breed of the 1960s that came to prominence by developing profit-making securities research for institutions and, as a result, actually buying the securities for these customers. "Before I knew it," she said, "I was making $150,000 a year as my share of the commissions." She then moved to partnerships with Stearns & Co., Finkle & Co., and Brimberg & Co., all member firms of the New York Stock Exchange, and was soon earning about $500,000 a year in commissions for her efforts.

In 1967 one of her customers, a prominent money manager, casually suggested to Miss Siebert that she buy a seat on the Exchange. "It took me about six months to get up my nerve," she said. "Only one person could be the first woman member of the stock exchange, but I wondered how having my own seat would affect my relationship with customers."

Once she had made up her mind to apply, Miss Siebert persisted and took the bold step of filing to become a member. As a partner in a member firm, she already was an allied member, but her application was for the real thing—full membership. The Exchange recognized that she was an outstanding candidate, with sizable financial resources, demonstrated ability, and a good track record in the industry. If her application were turned down, moreover, the Exchange would probably be accused of discrimination against women at a time when the women's liberation movement was gathering full steam. So the board approved Miss Siebert's membership in December 1967 and she paid $445,000 to purchase a seat. With the purchase came the coveted plastic-covered, white oval badge of a member—in this case bearing number 2646.

As president of the newly formed Muriel Siebert & Co., Mickie Siebert did not go on the floor too often, although she once said that "something I've always wanted to do [is go on the floor and] trade for my own account." But whenever she did leave her office to do business for her firm on the floor, she attracted attention—and not always of the positive kind—from the men there who were unaccustomed to a female presence in their midst.

In later years, Miss Siebert continued to do the unconventional, first forming an "execution-only" firm offering no research or investment advice but substantial discounts to institutional investors after brokerage commissions became fully negotiable in 1975. A year later, she became a discount broker for the public, again offering no investment opinions but, rather, rates that were 50 percent lower than the former fixed commission schedule. Business boomed, and Miss Siebert wound up answering the telephone herself on busy days to keep up with the demand. "We're a brokerage firm and people want to feel that you're there," she said. "It's not somebody calling up Bloomingdale's."

In 1977 Mickie Siebert was appointed to the prestigious post of Superintendent of Banks of New York State, placed the ownership of her firm in a blind trust, and left the securities industry. Many who knew her there thought that she would be back before too many years had passed.

Miss Siebert was joined on the Exchange by another woman in 1970, when Jane R. Larkin was elected to membership. Miss Larkin, a veteran in the securities business, who also spent most of her time in the office as an administrative partner rather than on the floor, paid about $180,000 for her seat. But when her employer, Hirsch & Co., was absorbed by Francis I. DuPont & Co., a larger member firm, a few months afterward, she gave up her membership, and until 1976 Miss Siebert again had the distinction of being the only woman member. During this interim, when many securities firms were having financial problems and seat sales plummeted, Miss Siebert was asked whether she would also sell her seat and replied, "I couldn't let the Exchange go back to being an all-male playground, could I?"

The first woman member who spent her full time on the floor arrived in 1976 in the person of Alice Jarcho, a thirty-year-old institutional broker for Oppenheimer & Co. Miss Jarcho arrived on the floor during a period when institutional volume provided the bulk of all trading there, and she quickly established herself as a pro among pros.

Ironically, it was Miss Larkin who played an important part in the development of Miss Jarcho's career, long before either became a member of the Exchange—and certainly representing no evidence of an "old girl" network in the financial community. Their paths first crossed in 1965, when Miss Jarcho took her first job after leaving college as a receptionist for Hirsch, where Miss Larkin was an executive.

Miss Jarcho left Hirsch after three months to become a secretary outside of Wall Street, but was contacted by Miss Larkin in 1967 with a proposal to work as the office secretary for a new branch that Hirsch had opened in mid-Manhattan. She remained there for two years, working as a troubleshooter and learning many of the facets of the brokerage business.

When Miss Jarcho felt that the time had come for her to do more complex work, she found a position as an order clerk for an arbitrageur at Oppenheimer. Her boss, Ted Fellerman, moved on to a couple of other concerns, including one of the predecessor firms of Shearson Loeb Rhoades, and took her with him as an associate.

At Shearson, Miss Jarcho's vocational aptitudes were recognized and she became first an institutional trader and then head of the trading desk for its investment advisory subsidiary, Bernstein-Macaulay. But her career took a giant leap forward in 1972 when she joined the Loews Corporation as a securities trader, working directly for a past master of the art, Laurence A. Tisch, chairman of the diversified insurance, tobacco, and hotel company.

"Working for a man like Larry Tisch was an incredible life and business experience," she said. "He gave me a tremendous amount of exposure to finance and gave me the opportunity to run my own department."

On October 1, 1976, after exactly four years at Loews, Miss Jarcho was hired by Oppenheimer as a vice-president, to become one of its five floor brokers at the Big Board. She spent a couple of weeks at the Oppenheimer office while completing the paper work required of all new Exchange members before purchasing a seat for $60,000 under an ABC agreement.

During her first day on the floor as a broker, proudly wearing her badge number 189, Miss Jarcho took a hard fall—literally rather than figuratively, and quite an embarrassing moment for a rookie. "I walked out of my booth in the morning to execute my first order," she recalled. "It was for ten thousand shares of the Franklin Mint, and my hand was shaking. I just took a few steps, slipped on a piece of paper, and fell right on my bottom. I guess I gave a couple of hundred people a good laugh. But I picked myself up and finished the execution."

By the time that Miss Jarcho became a floor broker on

the Big Board, most of the hostility toward and harassment of women as members that had greeted her predecessors had disappeared. "Some people, including some of the biggest names on the floor, have been extremely helpful and understanding," she observed. "Others couldn't understand why I left Loews or why Oppenheimer hired me."

Nevertheless, Alice Jarcho is satisfied with her role and her moneymaking opportunities on the floor of the Exchange. "Regardless of how many years you spend in this business, the floor is a completely different world," she noted. "There's a different verbiage, a different pace. You don't really know anything when you get here. Being on the floor is absolutely exhausting and draining. This is a staggering experience."

Miss Jarcho's appearance on the floor released the floodgates, and soon additional female members were accepted into the membership ranks. For instance, Ellen K. Lee, a twenty-five-year-old assistant vice-president of Bache Halsey Stuart Shields, became a floor member early in 1977 after having been a municipal bond trader for that firm. "When I graduated from Seton Hall University in 1974 and began to look for a career," she remarked, "I was initially offered three jobs—one as a model, one in retailing, and the lowest-paying as a trainee on Wall Street. I thought Wall Street was the place that had the most to offer, and I wasn't wrong."

Also in 1977, Myrna Skurnick, who works with her husband, Sam, a member of the Exchange, at his own company, bought a seat. The Skurnicks thereby became the first husband-and-wife team on the Exchange, joining the dozens of fathers and sons who have long been found working together on the floor and in the upstairs offices.

Mrs. Skurnick, however, sold her membership the following year.

Women are still a tiny minority of the 1,366 members of the Exchange, but they are no longer an oddity. Most newspapers do not now run lengthy feature stories each time a new woman is accepted for membership. Other floor brokers do not question their right to work alongside them and execute orders for their customers. The Exchange hierarchy is favorably disposed to their applications and encourages rather than discourages their membership.

Whether the day will come when women are represented on the floor even in proportion to their number in executive-level positions in business still remains to be seen. But until then, those women who are members ask to be judged on the basis of their performance rather than their sex. As Alice Jarcho puts it: "I have all the fears and trepidation of any person who first comes on the floor. But I have these feelings as a person, not as a woman. That's just an accident of birth."

17 TRADING FOR COMMISSIONS

It is 9:59 A.M., one minute before the market is to open for the day, and a red light appears on the big clock overlooking the floor of the New York Stock Exchange. The noise that has been building up for the last ten minutes gets louder, the movement of members from post to post gets faster, and the last of the files and records needed for the day's activities are put in place. Then at 10 A.M. the bell rings and all of the pent-up excitement bursts forth as trading begins and the first of the hundreds of millions of dollars' worth of securities that will change hands during the day are traded.

The flow of people and papers on the floor of the Exchange, along with the steady movement of the stock transaction tape listing all trades, continues until the market closes at 4 P.M. Then the bell rings again and trading ends. Members and employees leave the floor, but the process of reconciling orders and determining that the records are complete and accurate continues in the back offices. Some offices work through the night to be ready for the next day's opening at 10 A.M.

The most active members on the floor—physically active in terms of moving from place to place—are in most instances the commission brokers. Representing member firms, both large and small, they fill the buy and sell orders sent to their booths on the edge of the floor by taking them to the specialists' posts and attempting to obtain the best prices for their customers. Automation is now used to handle many of the small orders that are relatively simple to fill, but for those orders in which knowledge of the floor and skill in execution is an asset, the commission brokers play an important part. Here are some of them in action:

George H. Rose is a forty-six-year-old third-generation member of the New York exchange and a floor partner of Lazard Frères & Co. His grandfather was a two-dollar broker, an independent broker who executed orders for others on the floor. His father was a senior partner in DeCoppet and Doremus, a firm that dealt in "odd lots," or less-than-one-hundred-share units of trading, before that function was taken over by the Exchange itself. And George Rose and his brother Peter also became members when they grew to manhood.

"I started on the floor at fourteen, working summers," George Rose recalled. "I was terrified. One of my first recollections is when a man coming past our booth with a glass of water spilled it and caught me on the side of my seersucker suit."

A year after graduating from college in 1957, George Rose bought a seat on the Big Board and became an odd-lot broker with DeCoppet and Doremus. "It was and is basically a male society on the floor," he said. "And it's the most labor-intensive area in the world."

In 1968 Rose joined another firm, George Robinson & Company, where he specialized in trading big blocks of stocks for institutions like banks and insurance companies. Two years later he became the senior floor partner for White, Weld & Co. and remained there until 1975, when Lazard Frères & Co., the investment banking firm that traces its roots back to France, decided that it wanted a representative on the floor. It asked Rose to come aboard as its floor partner and he has been in that post ever since.

"We deal with large accounts," Rose said. Standing near a sign on a post that read THE SELLER MUST REPORT EACH TRANSACTION PROMPTLY TO THE REPORTER, he continued: "The other day I sold four hundred thousand shares of Johns-Manville. But whether it's a large or a small trade, there's no sense of isolation here. There is a collective sense of humor on the floor. It really is a people game."

In recent years, Rose has become involved in Exchange activities as a floor governor—an official who is sometimes called upon to solve disputes or handle problems that arise on a day-to-day basis. For example, governors have the power to halt trading in a stock when the specialist is swamped by a surge of buy or sell orders and cannot maintain an orderly market. Rose has had to handle that responsibility any number of times, and so when the electronic page that he carries in his breast pocket buzzes—indicating that he is wanted at his booth along the edge of the floor—the matter could just as well be Exchange business as it could be business for Lazard Frères.

Yet Rose enjoys his work and would not trade his life on the floor for any other line of business. "I can come down from lunch and know if the market is going up or down by the sounds I hear," he noted. "There's a totally different sound when the market is going up—it's electric. So I'm going to stay out there on the floor."

John A. Hirsch is, at forty years old, the senior floor partner of Bear, Stearns & Co. He is in charge of thirteen other Bear, Stearns brokers at the Big Board, two of whom are partners and eleven of whom are vice-presidents. The firm handles orders not only for its own customers, but also for 140 other brokerage firms for whom it acts as a "clearing" broker—responsible for executing orders and handling the accompanying paper work for the accounts that are sent by the originating firm. And Hirsch is right in the middle of all the action.

"It takes two to three years to learn the mechanics of the job down here," he said. "The difficult part is the market judgment, the market timing. That takes time."

Hirsch has been on the floor of the New York exchange for thirteen years and has the nuances down pat. After working for a while as a clerk, he bought a membership and has successively been an odd-lot broker, a specialist, and a two-dollar broker. But the job he likes best is the job he has now: that of a commission broker.

"You've got to be a 'salesman' on the floor too," he observed. "You have to talk to the salesmen at your firm and give them advice that they can pass along to their customers. A guy can't sit on his duff."

Hirsch is certainly not one to sit on his duff. Racing from post to post in his zone—Bear, Stearns divides the floor into twelve zones, which are given to different brokers to cover—and jumping into the other zones when difficulties arise, he is almost constantly in motion. "I check everything out that has to be checked out because a customer is involved," he said. "I don't care whether it's a one-hundred-share order or a one-hundred-thousand-share order."

When he is not on the go, Hirsch is likely to be standing near the turrets of telephones at his booth, talking to his office. For, in addition to the Teletype machines that print out orders transmitted from the Bear, Stearns order room to the Exchange's DOT system or execution of orders by the specialist, there are many direct telephone connections between the firm's headquarters and the floor. Beside those from the order room are connections leading to such key office locations as the block desk, the foreign department, the arbitrage department, and the desk that handles orders from client banks.

It took Hirsch less than a minute not too long ago to fill a customer's order to buy 7,000 shares of Inexco Oil, an oil and gas producer. The order came down as "18 top, not held," meaning that $18 a share was the highest price that would be paid and to use broker's discretion in the execution. Walking to the periphery of the crowd around the specialist's post (a sign nearby warns that MEMBERS NOT EXPECTING TO TRANSACT BUSINESS IN ACTIVE STOCKS ARE URGED TO ABSENT THEMSELVES FROM THE CROWD), he quickly learned that, in the specialist's book, 2,000 shares were available to buy at 17⅝ and 2,000 shares were available to sell at 17¾. Rather than call out his entire order and thereby risk the probability of forcing the price up, he made a series of trades in smaller units as other brokers came by the post to sell. The windup was the purchase of a total of 4,600 shares at 17⅞, 2,400 shares at 18, and a quick execution.

"It's funny, but the more volume you do, the less errors you usually have," Hirsch said. "When you're slow, minds start to wander and you get errors." But Hirsch feels that large volume will be the rule, rather than the exception, in the years ahead and that the legion of capable floor brokers will obtain the benefits of this trend. "People who are competitive and bright will survive," he added. "People who just hang out a shingle and hang on to this thing [pointing to his member's badge] will not."

"Remember that the New York Stock Exchange really started selling bonds, not stocks." The speaker is Walter J. McAdams, Jr., a director of the Garvin Bantel Corporation, a brokerage firm that specializes in bond trading, and he is talking about the Exchange's earliest sales and purchases of government bonds, which were then called stocks and were used to finance the new country's public debt. Mr. McAdams is Garvin Bantel's senior broker in the Big Board's bond room, which is a world of its own amid the stock exchange's emphasis on stocks.

The brown-carpeted room where McAdams spends his days is on the first basement level below the main trading floor on the ground level. Some two hundred people work in this 5,600-square-foot room, including members, clerks, and Exchange employees. Here is where close to three thousand different bond issues are traded in a manner vastly dissimilar from the way that stocks are bought and sold one floor above.

For bond brokers like McAdams don't deal with specialists when making a trade. The overwhelming bulk of the bonds listed on the Big Board are traded by means of the electronic Automated Bond System (ABS). Video display terminals are located around the room, through which a broker can determine the bid and asked prices and the number of $1,000 bonds in a particular category that other brokers would like to buy or sell. McAdams and his peers can punch in their buy or sell orders to the terminal and effect the trades automatically.

A few hundred bonds, however, principally convertibles and actively traded, volatile issues, are traded in what is called the active, or free, crowd, in a manner similar to that used at commodity exchanges. When McAdams has one of these bonds to trade, he determines the asked and offering prices, steps inside a brass railing that surrounds an octagonal trading pit, and places one foot in the pit to shout his bid. When another broker agrees to a trade, he also goes into the pit and indicates his acceptance of McAdams's proposal.

"At one time all bonds were traded on the floor," McAdams said. "But during the depression, interest rates were as low as 2 percent and members of the Exchange were charging $2.50 a bond. Gradually the bond market started to drift away, and most of it is now off the floor, although we trade a substantial amount here now."

Many bond traders at the Exchange, McAdams included, believe that theirs is the most fiercely competitive part of the securities business. "Sometimes when it gets hectic, the bar around the pit is pushed down and some members' and clerks' clothing gets ripped," he said. "Yet with all the competitiveness, there is a camaraderie here that exists nowhere else."

As far as Thomas F. Jessop is concerned, buying and selling stock on an exchange is "the only way for the little guy to get a fair price. In the over-the-counter market, the dealers can lengthen their spread [the difference between the bid and offer prices] and can walk away from a stock when they want [refuse to make trades in a security they previously traded]."

Jessop brings a bias to his analysis of the difference between exchange and over-the-counter trading, since he is the senior floor broker at the New York Stock Exchange for L. F. Rothschild, Unterberg, Towbin. But his experience of more than twenty years on the floor of both the Big Board and the American Stock Exchange has convinced him that customers on both sides of a transaction get the best shake when they trade in securities that are listed on an exchange.

"I once had an order to sell 16,000 shares of Eli Lilly," he said, "and the last sale was at 73¼. I found a buyer at the specialist's post who was willing to buy 10,000 shares at 73. Then the specialist bought 3,000 and we positioned the other 3,000 for our own account, also at 73. Later that day we sold those 3,000 shares at 73 and so we were clean."

Like so many other commission brokers, Jessop began his career as a page on the floor of the New York exchange. His next step up the ladder was as a clerk for a member firm, followed by the purchase of a seat on the American Stock Exchange in 1965. The following year, he joined Rothschild as a commission broker on the floor of the Amex, and in 1972 moved over to the New York Stock Exchange by buying a membership there.

"Like anything else, this is a game of personalities," said the thirty-nine-year-old Jessop, all the while keeping his eye on the annunciator board on the wall that flashes the numbers of brokers who are wanted at their booths. "There's also lots of action, and I like action."

Thus the hundreds of commission brokers on the floor of the Big Board run the gamut in experience, personality, and attitude. Each hopes to offer a unique advantage to his firm's customers by virtue of unusual talents or training. And in some cases a commission broker's special characteristics make him very much in demand.

For instance, Claude Sherman, a floor partner of Neuberger & Berman, was born in France and worked on the Paris Bourse before settling in the United States. He thus brings with him a detailed understanding of foreign securities and foreign arbitrage and provides his firm's clients with knowledge about these fields that can be extremely useful in their securities trading.

"The Bourse has no specialists because it's a call market," he said. "The brokers go to the trading post and an employee calls out the name of each stock for trades to be made. The New York Stock Exchange is a more effective market because it is continuous."

Sherman also considers the liquidity on the Big Board to be far greater than it is on the Bourse. "In France it's more of a dealer market, while in New York the spreads are closer and you can get in and out quicker."

Another commission broker with special talents of a very different kind is Paul L. Salembier, a vice-president of the First Boston Corporation. A former specialist and two-dollar broker, Salembier is an expert in handling institutional-size orders and is continually involved in his firm's positioning activities, when it buys from or sells to its customers in order to complete a big block transaction.

As he passed a specialist's post where a sign warns: CLERKS MUST NOT MAKE OR CONFIRM TRADES WITH MEMBERS, Salembier explained, "A good floor broker is as much responsible for positioning as the upstairs trader is. The floor broker gets a feel for whether the market is moving up or down and when to take a position in a stock. There are times when we are asked to make a bid or an offer that is suicidal. The floor broker is the eyes and ears of the traders upstairs and takes a big part in the pricing of the merchandise."

According to Salembier, the institutional customers who represent such a large percentage of Big Board trading are much more demanding now than they were in the past and are insisting on better executions from floor members. "So we try to give them various options about what to do in certain situations. We give them these alternatives and our recommendation and work together in making a decision."

Making decisions is what commission brokers do, in one way or another, for six hours a day. It is a pressure job, requiring great agility, and is not for the fainthearted. But for those who are successful it is filled with excitement and satisfaction every time a trade is completed at a better price or at a faster pace than might otherwise have been expected. These are the members of the Exchange to whom the word *broker* is most applicable, and their role seems destined to survive whatever the shape of the New York Stock Exchange in the 1980s and beyond.

18 MEMBERS AND THEIR PRANKS

Today the floor of the New York Stock Exchange is a busy center of trading activity. Rare is the moment when specialists, traders, commission brokers, and others on the floor have time on their hands to kill. With average daily trading volume in 1978 at 28.6 million shares and with turnover on peak days that year topping 60 million shares, normal activity on the floor is hectic. As a result, there is little opportunity for fun and games between 10 A.M. and 4 P.M.

Even if there were time, it is unlikely that there would be much of the type of prank that was so common two, three, and four decades ago. The business on the floor is much more serious, and although there is still a sense of comradeship there, it is not as great as it was in the past. Members do not, as they once did, tend to be from the same social set. Instead they range from clerks who "buy" a seat with funds provided by their employer to second- and third-generation scions of great wealth. Thus the old-school-tie atmosphere conducive to joshing and familiarity has largely disappeared.

The placement of millions of dollars' worth of electronic equipment on the floor has also precluded much of the horseplay of years gone by. Video display terminals, electronic card readers, and high-speed Teletype units, with extensive wiring to support them, are just some of the expensive gear on the floor used in connection with the plethora of systems that help to make the Exchange function—such as the ITS (Intermarket Trading System), DOT (Designated Order Turnaround) and ABS (Automated Bond System). A practical joke that goes astray could knock out a piece of this intricate equipment and cause severe damage to the processing of orders. And with enforcement of the rules against such jokes therefore stricter than it ever was, pranks and gags are few and far between.

But it was not always so. There were times when fun and games on the floor of the Exchange—and off the floor, too, by Exchange members—were virtually de rigueur. The old-timers who saw them happen remember this part of the past with great glee, while the younger members, who have heard the stories time and again, repeat them with equal enthusiasm. As one said, "These stories are as much a part of the Exchange heritage as the ticker tape."

One of the widely repeated stories, in one version or another, deals with putting a white powder on and around the shoes of an unsuspecting person, so that he will leave footprints wherever he goes on the floor. Talcum powder was traditionally placed at the feet of new members of the Exchange, men about to be married, and some of the visitors to the floor. Kirk Douglas, who was once given this treatment in the course of a VIP tour of the Exchange, first seemed to be upset and then bemused by the whole affair.

Another of the standard hazings given to new commission brokers and two-dollar brokers on the floor was the mock market in a fictitious stock. An elaborate procedure, involving perhaps a dozen brokers and specialists, would be set up whereby a bogus stock, stock symbol, specialist's book, and appurtenances would appear in order to trick the novice.

"The stock we created was a company called Transatlantic Bridge," recalled one old-timer. "Once we gave a new man an order to buy five thousand shares and sent him to a post where the crowd was bidding feverishly for the stock. He finally got the five thousand shares and came running back to the booth, when we told him he made a mistake—he was supposed to have sold five thousand shares. So he went racing back again to sell the five thousand he had bought and the five thousand he was supposed to have sold. When he was all finished, someone threw a bag of water at him, everybody laughed, and that was the end of it."

Many outsiders might call the high jinks on the floor sophomoric, and to some extent they are right. Grown men shooting water pistols at each other in a business setting or spilling water on someone's seat are not practices taught at graduate schools of business. Yet the genesis of what seems to be silly could very well be the extreme tension that floor members of the New York Stock Exchange are subjected to each day. Often they must write one thing, speak another, and think a third at the same time, all the while concentrating on not making a mistake that could cost thousands or tens of thousands of dollars. After days on end of such mental strain, it is not surprising that efforts are made to relieve the built-up pressure through the safety valve of mirth and silliness.

For example, there was the time that two members had such an intense hatred of each other that almost everyone on the floor was aware of the feud. A few brokers decided to test that mutual dislike by sneaking up behind them when they were near each other in a crowd around a specialist's post and handcuffing them together. The denouement of this story—after the two brokers were forced to spend hours not only in such close proximity but uncomfortably as well—depends on the recollection of the storyteller. Some say that the handcuffs had to be sawed off after the close of trading, while others report that the two had to share a cab to a midtown New York hotel where the keys to the handcuffs had been left at the front desk. In either case, the two feuding members were forcibly made aware that absence makes the heart grow fonder.

Another humorous situation involved a broker who was extremely unpopular among the members on the floor because of his generally antagonistic disposition. When he stepped out to the smoking room just off the floor, he would always sit in the same chair unless it was already occupied. When it was, the broker would sit across the aisle from that chair in a telephone booth, preventing others from using the phone and glowering at the person in "his" chair until he felt uncomfortable and left. A half-dozen members obtained retribution one day when the broker was glowering in the phone booth by slamming the door shut and taping it so that it could not be opened from the inside. The laughter could be heard back on the floor.

Ed Anderson, who was a member for many years, recalled how he celebrated his twenty-first birthday on the floor in 1934. "I stood at my post to pick up the telephone, and when I held it close to my ear, it was covered with red ink. Then I smelled a terrible smell. Someone had spilled a bottle of cheap perfume on my suit and I had to live with it all day. In those days it was dull on the floor, the ticker tape might stop for twenty minutes, and there was time for this."

There was time for more fun on the floor in many other ways. For instance, there were always a few moments for song. In the 1930s the unofficial theme of the floor became "Wait 'Til the Sun Shines, Nelly"—a melody that to this present day brings forth smiles of recognition of "our song" from dozens of members.

Whether it is because of the original symbolism during the depression, the strong Irish influence on the floor, or the need for a rallying cry, "Wait 'Til the Sun Shines, Nelly" caught on and just about everyone sang it. For many years a group of brokers gathered at 2:15 P.M. (then the delivery time for trades made the previous day) at Post 11 to sing a few verses after another group of members had sung "The Wearing of the Green." Nelly won out in popularity, and afterward it was also sung whenever a momentous—or what seemed at the time to be momentous—occasion arose on the floor. Perhaps its final significant rendition on the floor was given on May 21, 1976, the last day that odd lots were traded by odd-lot brokers. At noon that day, every member who was at one time an odd-lot broker—the number runs into the dozens —and the remaining odd-lotters gathered together for a soulful rendition. The song is still sung at the Exchange's annual golf outing, however, especially when the tales start to flow about the good old days.

There were also other songs that worked their way into the floor's repertoire for one reason or another. In the television heyday of the Mickey Mouse Club, a group of members decided that one of the floor brokers looked like the famous Walt Disney creation. So every afternoon for months on end they would appear before him and sing in unison, "M-I-C-K-E-Y M-O-U-S-E" and the rest of the theme from that program. Another member was named MacNamara and was therefore serenaded periodically on the floor with a rendition of "MacNamara's Band." John S. Karger, the chairman of Rothschild Securities Corporation, who spent thirty-eight years on the floor, recalled that because some brokers thought he looked Chinese, they would serenade him periodically to the tune of "Chinatown." Exchange authorities finally put a stop to chorusing on the floor, terming it below the dignity of such an august body.

George C. Dinsmore, a veteran specialist with Stokes, Hoyt & Company, remembers a less pleasant effort to loosen the tension. "One day someone dropped a tear-gas bomb down the air-conditioning shaft . . . around twelve noon," he said. "You would have to be there to appreciate the effect. Within seconds the floor was cleared and the specialist books and papers had to be removed at the same time."

Another floor tradition that remains in the fond memory of many of the members is the dressing up by some brokers as well-known personalities. One of the most frequently recalled incidents arose in the 1930s when a broker by the name of John Murray was an independent candidate for membership on the Exchange board of governors. An ardent Democrat, he appeared one day in the visitors gallery overhanging the floor with Alfred E. Smith, the former Governor of New York and Democratic presidential hopeful, to help him win votes. In an attempt to poke fun at this effort, a second broker appeared soon thereafter in the same visitors gallery with his arm around a man dressed like Mahatma Gandhi, the Indian leader, who waved to the brokers below as Smith had done. At least partly as a result of this parody of the Smith endorsement, Murray did not come close to winning the board membership. Other personages who have been impersonated on and around the floor by members include Emperor Haile Selassie of Ethiopia and the ever-popular Santa Claus.

In the days when seriousness was not the watchword it is today, any member with a distinguishing trait or characteristic of any kind was subject to public ridicule, although usually in a friendly manner. One was Henry Sternberg, a specialist and a general in the National Guard, who was frequently taunted by the former privates on the floor. As it happens, he once grabbed a taunter, Phil Green, by the arm and pulled it hard. Green wasn't hurt, but pretended to be injured and appeared on the floor shortly thereafter with his arm in a sling. Sternberg was terribly upset and gave Green one hundred dollars to pay for his medical bills, whereby the "injured" man pulled off the sling and announced that the money would be used for a party for the entire group around the post. And so it was.

A veteran broker remembered a very special specialist with a flair by the name of Ollie Campbell. "He always wore a wing collar, a wig, and a felt hat on the floor, and he was known as a salmon fisherman," he said. "Someone once brought a fishing pole and hooked his hat and wig off. Campbell went rushing around the place all perturbed."

Still another trick involving hats pulled on a member dealt with the broker who wore a stiff straw hat to work during the summer and always hung it on a particular hook in the coatroom. As a practical joke, some of his colleagues learned that his hat size was 7 and therefore bought exactly the same hat in a half-dozen other sizes, such as 6¾, 7¼, and 7½. Then they began substituting one or another of the wrong-sized hats for the right one on the hook, so that the broker would be inexplicably faced with a different poorly-fitting hat every day. It took him a week or so to figure out what was going on, but when he did, he laughed as loudly as the culprits.

Jacob C. Stone, another floor veteran and partner in the specialist firm of Asiel & Company, told of the time when three of the tallest men on the floor, Stuyvesant Fish, William Vaughn, and Howard Foster, had some fun at the expense of one of the shortest. The three members, all six feet, five inches tall, grabbed a man who was just over five feet tall and carried him in their arms through the room while singing songs. They never received a reprimand, Mr. Stone said, but they never did it again.

Incidents like these, of course, were the exception rather than the rule. Even during the long dull periods when daily trading volume was under a million shares a day, there was more boredom than excitement. There were times when a bowling ball would be rolled down an aisle to see if the members were on their toes. And there were times when a backgammon set would be pulled out at a specialist's post and two brokers would have a go at it. But more likely there would be joke telling, newspaper and book reading, and other less hectic pursuits when the action on the floor tapered off.

Nevertheless the legends of the pranksters on the floor live on. Some are likely to be apocryphal stories that have been embellished through the years. Others are likely to be partially rooted in truth and partially in exaggeration. But many of these tales symbolize a period whose time is largely past—a period of a gentlemen's club when some members would tease others in wild, woolly ways and would be teased in return, all in good fun. The modern era on the floor does not allow for such fun, and the members are probably the losers for it.

19

FIRST STEPS
ON THE ROAD
TO RICHES

Not every member on the floor of the New York Stock Exchange was once a clerk or page who worked his way up. But dozens of the present members achieved success after carrying messages or transcribing orders on the same floor where they are now exercising the judgment and discretion called for in their positions. And dozens of the current force of uniformed men and women on the floor have similar dreams of earning a six-figure income as one of the 1,366 members of the Exchange.

For the floor is one of the few important places left in American business where enormous status, prestige, and salary can be realized without the benefit of a college education or a family influence. Doctors, lawyers, senior executives at large corporations, and most other top-ranking officials in industry and finance require at least a college degree, and probably a graduate degree too, for entry into the field and for movement into the front ranks. The floor also has its share of graduates from Ivy League and other colleges, as well as a sprinkling of men with graduate degrees in economics or business administration. Yet there are enough members on the floor, young and old, who do not hold any degrees to indicate that the opportunity is open to anyone who wants to try to parlay ambition, determination, skill, and luck into a membership on the Big Board.

The cadre of employees now working on the floor consists of about a thousand men and women with various backgrounds and aptitudes. Not all, of course, want to become members some day, with many viewing their present jobs as a means of earning a living and nothing more. A look at some of them as they go about their work, relax in the Exchange cafeteria, or stand outside the building during their rest periods presents a picture in microcosm of the people who operate the facilities on the floor of the Exchange.

Frank Harnisher is a thirty-seven-year-old order clerk on the floor for the specialist firm of deCordova, Cooper & Co. Like about half of the employees on the floor, Harnisher works for a member firm rather than for the Exchange itself. He wears a light cream-colored jacket— the uniform for specialist clerks—as he stands for more than six hours alongside five other deCordova, Cooper clerks in the center of the horseshoe-shaped Post 10 where his company makes a market in about ten stocks.

Harnisher, who is married and has four children, came to work on the floor in 1959, after graduating from high school and working for three years for Citibank. "My father worked here and so did my father's father, so coming down to the floor was really a challenge for me," he said. "I was scared, and it took a few months until I knew what I was doing."

The greatest difficulty faced by Harnisher on his arrival at the floor was similar to that faced by all new specialist clerks—the language of the investment world. "One specialist said that the market in a stock was 'a-quarter-three-quarters' [one quarter bid and three quarters offered] and

I thought he said, 'Give me the order.'" Another problem for Harnisher was learning to write fractions in the specialists' books as it is done on the floor without a line between the numerator and the denominator.

Harnisher's first job was as a clerk for John Muir & Co., where he remained for a year and a half. Then deCordova, Cooper offered him more money and a better opportunity for future progress, so he switched over to its Post 10. Harnisher is now the firm's head clerk and earns $365 a week plus a Christmas bonus.

"It's hard keeping up with the pressure in an active market," he said. "And I'm a little bit leery about automation coming in. The business is changing every day from what we used to know."

Unlike most floor employees, who work from just before the market opening at 10 A.M. to just after the closing at 4 P.M.—with a lunch and a rest break thrown in—Harnisher, as the senior clerk, puts in a full business day. He arrives at the deCordova, Cooper office at 20 Exchange Place each weekday morning at 9 A.M. to gather the specialists' books, daily statements of their holdings in each stock traded, and other pertinent material for the partners before going onto the floor a half hour later to prepare for the opening. After the close, he is responsible for winding up the paper work on the floor before returning to the office at 4:30 P.M. for a final hour's work sorting out the hundreds of pieces of paper that identify the day's trading done by the specialists for whom he works.

"At the end of the day, it's a pleasure to get back to the office and sit down," he noted. "But I still prefer to be busy than bored. When you're bored, you make a lot more mistakes."

Harnisher's big hope is that lightning will strike and he

will be asked to become a junior partner of the firm that has employed him for more than eighteen years, just as it happened to Thomas Schwalenberg, who preceded him as chief clerk. In a blunt way, he gives voice to his dream: "I want to make a good buck. That's what I'm here for."

Salvatore Celi is nineteen years old, single, and a page based at Post 7 on the floor of the Exchange. Pages, who wear light-blue jackets for identification, fall into two categories: carrier pages, who collect from floor reporters the computer cards containing the latest sales information, and squad pages, who assist commission brokers at their booths and elsewhere on the floor. Celi has been a carrier page for more than two years.

"My cousin works here as a floor reporter and I put in an application when I graduated high school," he said. "After being here for a while as a page, I went to work for a specialist firm for a couple of months, but it didn't work out, so I came back."

Celi's goal is to become a floor reporter—the person who transcribes each trade as it occurs on a computer card that pages take to terminals for electronic transmission to the ticker tape listing every transaction. His major reason is that a floor reporter's starting salary is $250 a week, double the $125-a-week starting salary of a page.

"The chance of becoming a reporter is a good opportunity for me," Celi said. "I'll have to take three written tests and a floor test first. But that's what I want to do."

When William Gilberti was eighteen years old, he answered a help-wanted advertisement in the New York *Times* for a position as a page on the floor of the New York Stock Exchange. Now it is twenty years later, and

Gilberti is still working on the floor, wearing the required black jacket of a tube clerk.

The job of a tube clerk is to relay messages and orders from slots at the brokers' booths around the perimeter of the floor to the specialists' posts in the center through the Exchange's pneumatic tube system. Many brokers use the tubes to send buy and sell limit orders to the specialists, who also use them to report back on the execution of these orders. In addition, requests and responses dealing with quotations and other market information are transmitted through the miles of pneumatic tubes buried under the floor of the three ground-level rooms where the trading is done.

"I didn't think I'd be here this long when I joined the Exchange," Gilberti reflected. "I went to college for three years at night, but then I quit and here I am."

Soon after Gilberti was hired by the Exchange, he was promoted from a page to a quote boy, which required him to spend the day on the telephone calling stock quotations from the floor to the upstairs office. This information was collected each time a specialist made a quotation change following a transaction. But the quote boy job was eliminated with the computerization of quotation information, and Gilberti became a tube clerk fifteen years ago.

"The big advantage of this job is that I'm able to work independent of other people's personalities," he said. "But it can be boring when trading is slow."

John DiGiglio also followed the path from page to quote boy, but he became a floor, or sales, reporter fourteen years ago and has remained one ever since. At the age of thirty-four, with seventeen years of service on the floor, he knows that the Exchange is definitely his career.

"The Exchange tries to equal the weekly wages of specialist clerks in its upper-level floor jobs like mine," DiGiglio said. "But the clerks get higher bonuses at Christmas and they have a chance of becoming a member."

Many pages, reporters, and tube men are asked by specialists to work as their clerks, particularly when a floor employee is noticed for application to duty or speed in accomplishing his tasks. But not all of those who accept a clerk's position find it to their liking or within their capacity, so the Exchange gives them six months to return from such an experiment without any loss of seniority.

The fact that only six working hours are required from most of the Exchange's floor employees makes DiGiglio's job very appealing to him. "And if you have an interest in the market and follow its activity, the job can be exciting and stimulating," DiGiglio added.

DiGiglio, who also wears the Exchange's black jacket in his job, admitted, however, that there are a number of disadvantages to a floor reporter's work. "You can get lost in the shuffle if you're not promoted," he noted. "And you stand in one spot all day long, so you have to keep alert to catch all of the trades that are made."

There are certain compensations to a floor employee's job, regardless of whether or not it leads to a much higher level, according to DiGiglio. First there are the famous people he has seen on the floor, such as actors James Stewart and Kirk Douglas and quarterbacks Y. A. Tittle and Fran Tarkenton. "Even Richard Nixon came down here to shake hands after he lost [the race for] the governorship of California in 1962," he said.

A conspicuous development on the floor in recent years is the relatively large number of women who have been employed by the Exchange at this formerly all-male bastion. One of these women is Jo Ann Piccirillo, a twenty-one-year-old page who has worn the light-blue smock that serves as identification for women pages for a year and a half.

"I'd like to become a specialist clerk," she said. "You go into a firm and they teach you the basics of the business. Some firms have already spoken to me, but the salary wasn't that good or I didn't think the firm was that good."

Miss Piccirillo worked for a short time in an office before being hired as a page, and jumped at the opportunity to move away from a desk job when the Exchange called her after she filed an application. "It's a pleasure to work on the floor," she explained. "You meet a lot of nice people and you get around a lot."

Apparently less motivated than Miss Piccirillo is Eugene Barbosa, a twenty-four-year-old page who has been employed on the floor since he was sixteen years old and a student in the co-op program at Seward Park High School on the Lower East Side of Manhattan. While a student, he attended school and worked at the Exchange on alternate weeks; after graduating in 1969, he stayed on. His salary as a page based at Post 12 was then $70 a week and is now $145.

Although the usual upward progression of jobs on the floor has been from page to tube clerk to reporter, Barbosa decided to bypass the tube clerk slot and wait until he can become a reporter. "I'd rather walk around as a page than shove papers in tubes," he said. "A lot of people don't like that job, but they're making $200 or $250 a week and they need the money."

Barbosa has no aspirations to become a member of the

Exchange. "I've been here too long and I wouldn't make the Exchange my career," he asserted. "My back used to bother me a lot until I got used to it. I just work my six hours a day and that's that.

"You know, it would have been nice to think of being a member if I had any interest in it. But the way the market is going, there's no security even there. And if you're the low man on the totem pole, when the firm gets into trouble you're the first one to go."

The employees who work on the floor of the Exchange are both happy and unhappy with their jobs, ambitious for higher positions and satisfied with what they have, hoping against hope to become a member someday and not caring whether the chance ever arises. Depending upon their individual abilities and inclinations, they are hardworking or dilatory, assertive or compliant, gifted or lacking more than the elementary skills needed for entry-level jobs.

Yet what makes the floor different from so many other aspects of American business at the dawn of the 1980s is the *opportunity* for advancement to a powerful and lucrative post, regardless of origin or education. Employees have so many role models around them of former workers who achieved success as members that they can identify with them and have legitimate aspirations to follow in their footsteps. And as long as the workers on the floor can aspire to membership and some of them are fortunate enough to reach it, the New York Stock Exchange will continue to be a magnet for young people everywhere who still want to relive the Horatio Alger legend for themselves.

PART V

The Floor
of Tomorrow

20

TOWARD THE NINETEEN-EIGHTIES AND BEYOND

Today's high-ceilinged floor of the New York Stock Exchange is a far cry from the area around the buttonwood tree on Wall Street where trading first began in 1792. And the floor of the future, wherever it is and however it functions, is likely to be much different from the arena now operating at the corner of Broad and Wall streets. The change between today and tomorrow, moreover, is likely to be just as dynamic as previous changes, although the time frame may be considerably less.

For slowly—too slowly to suit some members of Congress and the Securities and Exchange Commission—the Big Board and the other securities exchanges are traveling in the direction of a national market system. Its outlines are broad enough to allow plenty of room for inclusion of all kinds of stock trading, on exchange floors as well as on the over-the-counter market. Yet there seems to be little doubt that the New York exchange will be a major participant in this "floor" of tomorrow, whether it is a physical entity or an electronic linkage bringing together market makers from all over the country.

The present trading floor traces its origins back to 1903, when the present structure, afterward connected to an office building, was erected in the center of the financial district. Twenty-one years later, the main trading floor was extended by an addition at the northern end facing Wall Street, usually called by floor members "the garage." In 1969 still another section for trading was added, with the opening of the contiguous eight-thousand-square-foot "blue room" to the south. The blue room's design was more modernistic than the standard multi-post layout of the other rooms and from the outset has contained such accoutrements as two giant horseshoe posts for all trading, computer-operated price display boards, and a closed-circuit television system. Ten years later, another $12 million was being spent to update the floor facilities with electronic systems and more modern trading posts.

All of these additions and developments were, however, based on the traditional trading floor concept—a single enclosed area in New York to which orders, both buy and sell, must be brought for execution. But the trend now is in the direction of an electronic link of a variety of securities markets in some manner that will allow customers, through their brokers, to buy and sell at any exchange. With this electronic connection, a broker could easily choose exchanges in Boston or Philadelphia, according to the theory, if he believes that he will be able to get as good (or better) a price and execution as at the New York Stock Exchange.

"The uncertainty over lack of structure of the national market system is the biggest single millstone around the industry's neck," said Robert C. Hall, former executive vice-president of the Big Board. "But we should use the New York Stock Exchange system as a foundation for whatever comes next."

Yet the members on the floor of the New York exchange are moving more with deliberate speed than with haste toward the floor of the future. Each step has to be explained and reexplained, as they see the familiar procedures of the past being replaced by new electronic methodology that in many cases is still an unknown quantity. Nevertheless, most of them recognize the necessity of adapting to these changes, if for no other reason than self-interest. For if they do not lead the way toward a trading system linking or combining other markets with their own, it will probably be done for them by the Securities and Exchange Commission—and certainly on terms not as much to their liking.

The essentials of the national market system proposal of the New York Stock Exchange are simple: each exchange and the over-the-counter market would remain an independent entity, but would be joined electronically for the purpose of establishing procedures and programs for linked trading. In contrast to those in Washington and elsewhere who want the end result of national market planning to be a unitary central market, the Big Board theoreticians have always backed a system in which the diversity of approaches, interests, and capabilities among the market centers can be maintained instead of eradicated. Rather than a "black box" (the pejorative for a single all-electronic system) or even a "white box" (this system envisioned in a more benign manner), the New York exchange is promoting an intermarket system as its target for the future.

Some of the ingredients of such a system have long been there: a consolidated transaction-reporting service, a national clearance and settlement system, and a composite quotation system. But the focus of this plan is the Intermarket Trading System—conceived by the New York

Stock Exchange and now electronically linking it and the American Stock Exchange, the Boston Stock Exchange, the Midwest Stock Exchange in Chicago, the Philadelphia Stock Exchange, and the Pacific Stock Exchange in Los Angeles and San Francisco. The ITS allows a broker at one exchange to reach electronically into another to execute an order if a better price exists there. A central minicomputer facilitates the routing of orders and confirmations among them, while cathode ray terminals and accompanying hardware are strategically located on each floor for sending and receiving messages.

On these terminals, moreover, are flashed not only the particular stock quotations from the participating exchanges, but also the size of the offering. Individual specialist quotation displays show their own bids and offers, plus those of the best market in the ITS, along with an identifier for the Exchange. If an order is entered into this system but not acted upon within a prescribed time limit, it is automatically canceled. Confirmations and cancellations are also printed at the station on the floor at which the information was initially entered. In addition, quotation displays are continuously updated throughout the system.

For example, if a floor member of the New York Stock Exchange receives an order from a customer to buy one hundred shares of a stock that is also listed on the Pacific and Philadelphia exchanges, he will go to the post at which that stock is traded and ask, "What's the market?" The specialist may respond, "40, ¼," meaning that the best bid to buy is 40 and the best offer to sell is 40¼. By glancing at the quotation display above the post, however, the commission broker may see that there is a better offer to sell by the specialist on the Pacific Stock Exchange, whose price is 40⅛. As a result, the New York exchange broker would then electronically send a firm commitment to buy to the Pacific specialist at that price. If the 40⅛ offer is still available in the few moments that it takes for this commitment to reach the West Coast, the specialist there would accept the commitment and execute the order. Within seconds, the confirmation would be printed out at a terminal on the New York floor as evidence of the transaction and the order would be shown on the consolidated tape.

Once the ITS became part and parcel of the floor operations at the New York Stock Exchange, the next step was the linking of limit orders. For instance, if a stock was trading at 50, a customer might enter an order to sell at 52 or to buy at 48.

The Big Board's way of expanding and enhancing the data processing and communications availability for limit orders was to conceptualize a series of limit order files at each securities exchange. With this open display of public limit orders, brokerage firms would be able to enter, cancel, or obtain the status of limit orders in the files directly from their offices. The files would open the traditionally secret specialist's book and give full knowledge of all entered limit orders to the participants at the various exchanges.

With such electronic limit order files, each exchange would be able to display throughout the entire system the limited price orders that its specialists hold. All of these orders at any given exchange would be joined together in an electronic composite display—similar to the composite quotation systems already existing—so that everyone in the system would know about each order. Furthermore, this type of display might make it easier to trade blocks via the Intermarket Trading System because "upstairs" block traders would immediately become aware of what orders in the specialist's book must be satisfied before any transaction can be completed outside the composite quotation.

The major alternative to this series of limit order files as the foundation of the floor of tomorrow is the central limit order file proposed by the SEC. This file was described by the commission as "a mechanism in which public limit orders can be entered and queued for execution in accordance with the auction trading principles of price and time priority and by means of which such orders can be assured of receiving an execution prior to the execution of any other order by a broker in any market at the same or an inferior price." For the most part, members of the Big Board rose up in arms against this kind of mechanism, terming it an abandonment of the public that the federal watchdog agency was pledged to serve.

This central limit order file, or CLOF, "is a monolithic entity with absolute time priority across markets," said one floor member. Among the disadvantages of CLOF cited by him and other members was its discrimination in favor of public limit orders and against all other public orders. And since limit orders are a distinct minority of all public orders on exchanges, this discrimination appeared to these critics to be in favor of a minority, not the majority, of orders.

Big Board floor members asserted, moreover, that the CLOF might subordinate all other trading strategies to the prepricing of orders and entering them into the file. Other criticisms were: (1) it might restrict competition by creating a single uniform market for limit orders with advantages that could not be matched by those trading otherwise; (2) it might adversely affect the trading process because of the difficulty of integrating an electronic file with an auction trading crowd; and (3) its quality of service might be seriously disappointing to even its major proponents.

"With CLOF, there would be neither competition among orders, competition among market makers, nor competition among market centers," said one floor broker. "Innovation would be smothered, and nobody wants that."

For whatever its flaws have been in the past—and admittedly there have been many—the New York Stock Exchange has always offered investors an auction market—one in which there is competition among orders to buy and sell in a single marketplace. The complications of limit orders and other stock market techniques to limit losses have eliminated the ideal model of the past. Nevertheless, prices arrived at between buyers and sellers do reflect the forces of supply and demand in the marketplace, while economies of scale are achieved by virtue of the institutional-size block orders that interact with the round-lot orders from small investors.

The New York exchange's limit order file system is obviously designed to retain the traditional role of the Big Board specialist in facilitating trading with minimal disturbances to this auction process. Specialists are not free to buy and sell at will, since they have the obligation to maintain orderly price movements. Specialists have the opportunity to be dealers, rather than agents, only when their quotes fall between the bid and asked prices of public orders. As the Big Board members see it, the public benefits from these self-regulatory controls and will continue to do so under the automated processes that are developed.

The New York Stock Exchange's national market system proposal thus seeks a measure of balanced competition among the exchanges and the over-the-counter market. But this competition requires best-market pricing of orders, developed as competitive exchanges fight for business from commission brokers. Since developments that reduce the scope of auction trading—such as internalization, or in-house trading by large retail-oriented firms directly with their customers—do the opposite, the Exchange has fought to prevent them from taking hold. The jury is still out on internalization, but what is certain is that, if spreads between bid and asked prices widen, the professionals in the business will benefit to the detriment of the public. And most members of the New York Stock Exchange recognize that such a course, while immediately profitable, is in the long run self-defeating.

As might have been expected, the announcement of the New York exchange's limit order file plan was not universally accepted. Some saw it as fragmentation, others as a way to dissipate the SEC's original intention of spurring the securities industry to develop a consolidated limit order book for all exchanges. Nevertheless, working within a framework of the Securities Acts Amendments of 1975, the Big Board is attempting to lay the groundwork for a file system for public limit orders at the different market centers that would receive input from member firms both on and off the floor of the Exchange. Executions, of course, could be accomplished only by the specialist.

From the floor members' point of view, orders in this limit order facility would have the same priority that limit orders in the specialist's book have always enjoyed. What's more, public limit orders could be entered at the New York Stock Exchange by brokers and dealers on other exchanges, thereby offering the opportunity for additional revenues. And this, in turn, might very well lead to the protection of limit orders across competing exchanges.

The rationale for such protection is that an individual or institution leaving a limit order at one exchange should have a guarantee that it will not be executed at inferior prices to those at another exchange. There must be assurances, therefore, that no transaction will occur within the confines of this interlinked system that will not first satisfy limit orders at a better price anywhere in the system. The Big Board board of directors has let the members know in no uncertain terms that they must go to another exchange when the limit order files are in operation if a better price for their customers is available there. And although this means the possibility of siphoning off volume now on the New York exchange, the financial strength and sagacity of its floor members are an indication that there is just as much, if not more, likelihood that the flow of orders will over the long run be in their direction.

For this is what the floor of the New York Stock Exchange is all about: what it is, what it has been, and what it will be. For close to two hundred years, the brokers and traders there have lived by their wits by buying for themselves and their customers at a lower price and selling at a higher one than traders elsewhere. They were successful in doing so in the days of the quill pen and they are successful in the days of the computer terminal. Tomorrow's floor still has hundreds of question marks surrounding it, but if history is any guide, the members of the Big Board will move up to and into the twenty-first century wielding new strategies and tactics that will help them not only survive, but also prosper in the years ahead.

GLOSSARY

ABC AGREEMENT An agreement between a member of the New York Stock Exchange and the firm he or she works for, through which the funds to purchase a membership are provided by the firm even though the seat is in the individual's name. If the member wishes to sell this seat, he or she must first purchase it from the firm or arrange for the firm to be otherwise compensated.

ARBITRAGE A technique sometimes used by stock market professionals that takes advantage of a temporary price difference in related securities. The type most frequently practiced today is risk arbitrage, which involves the purchase of securities expected to be valued higher in the future because a potential acquirer may offer a premium over the market price.

AUCTION MARKET The type of market on the floor of the New York Stock Exchange where bidders vie against each other to purchase and sell securities.

BEAR MARKET A period characterized by a long-term trend of sharply declining prices.

BID AND ASKED Also called quotation or quote. The bid price for a security is the highest price that anyone is willing to offer at a particular time. The asked price is the lowest price that anyone is willing to accept for this same security at the same time. The actual price at which the deal is done is usually between the bid and asked prices.

BIG BOARD The expression widely used on Wall Street to refer to the New York Stock Exchange. The exchange is also known as the NYSE.

BLACK TUESDAY October 29, 1929, when a record number of shares for that period were traded on the New York Stock Exchange and prices began a tumultuous decline. Considered to be the outset of the crash of 1929 and the start of the Great Depression.

BLUE CHIP The common stock of a widely known, profitable company that pays regular dividends.

BOND An IOU or promissory note of a corporation or government used as evidence of an obligation that the issuer promises to repay at a specified interest rate and during a specified period of time. Most bonds pay interest on a regular periodic basis.

BULL MARKET A period characterized by a long-term trend of sharply advancing prices.

COMMON STOCK A security that represents an ownership interest in a corporation.

CORNER Buying a stock on a scale large enough to give the purchaser or purchasing group control over the price. With this power over the supply of a particular stock held by others, buyers who sold short must now obtain the shares to cover their positions at terms dictated by the controlling group.

CROWD The group of brokers gathered around a trading post on the floor of the New York Stock Exchange who buy or sell shares traded there.

DEBENTURES A corporate bond backed by the general credit of its issuer and not secured by a mortgage or lien on specific property. Debentures are the most common type of bond issued by large, well-established corporations with good credit ratings.

FLOOR REPORTER An employee of the New York Stock Exchange who stands outside the trading posts and notes each sale on cards that are electronically scanned for transmittal to the ticker tape on which prices are printed on a current basis.

INSTITUTIONAL INVESTOR A buyer of securities in large quantities: a major institution like a mutual fund, pension fund, or insurance company.

INTERMARKET TRADING SYSTEM An electronic system linking the floors of the New York Stock Exchange and five other stock exchanges in the United States, enabling a broker on one floor to execute orders through a computer at any of the other participating market centers.

LEVERAGE The effect on per-share earnings of a corporation's common stock when large amounts must be paid first for bond interest or dividends on preferred stock.

LIMIT ORDER An order to buy or sell a specified number of shares of a security at a specified price or better.

MARGIN BUYING Buying securities by using the broker's credit as partial payment. The money put up by the broker is called the margin.

MARKET ORDER An order to buy or sell a specified number of shares of a security at the most advantageous current price after the order reaches the floor of the New York Stock Exchange.

ODD LOT Any amount traded that differs from the conventional unit of trading or a multiple thereof. In most instances, this means fewer than one hundred shares, which comprise a round lot.

OPTION The right to buy or sell a specific number of shares of an underlying security at a fixed, or striking, price before the expiration date. An option to buy is termed a *call* and an option to sell is called a *put*.

ORDER CLERK Employees of specialist firms who stand inside the trading posts on the floor of the New York Stock Exchange and help maintain the specialists' books and records.

OVER-THE-COUNTER MARKET The arena for trading stocks and bonds that are not listed on the New York Stock Exchange or other organized securities exchanges. The over-the-counter market is not a physical location but consists largely of a communications network of dealers who trade for their own accounts through negotiation.

PAGE An employee of the New York Stock Exchange who assists brokers on the floor.

PREFERRED STOCK A security that represents an owner-ship interest in a corporation and also gives its owner a prior claim over common stock on the company's earnings and assets. Called a senior security, preferred stock is nor-mally entitled to a specific dividend payable every year before dividends can be paid to common stockholders.

PRICE-EARNINGS RATIO The current market price of a share of stock divided by the corporation's per-share earn-ings for a twelve-month period. A yardstick of value for in-vestors, it is also known as the *P-E ratio*.

SEAT A membership on the New York Stock Exchange giv-ing its owner the right to buy and sell securities there. The expression dates back to the Exchange's earliest days, when members sat in the Tontine Coffee House transacting their business.

SELLING SHORT Selling securities that a person does not own, with the expectation that their market value will decline and the seller will be able to buy them at a lower price and make a profit. Short sales are now regulated by the Federal Reserve Board and the New York Stock Ex-change.

SPECIALIST A member of the New York Stock Exchange who helps to maintain a fair and orderly market by buying and selling for his own account and also acts as a broker's broker in the handling of limit orders. Specialists confine their activities to a particular group of stocks bought and sold around the perimeter of their trading post.

SPECIALIST'S BOOK A book maintained by a specialist for each stock he handles in which limit orders are listed until they are executed.

SYNDICATE An organization of investment bankers formed to market a new securities issue or a large block of an outstanding issue. Also called an *underwriting group* or *selling group*.

TRADING POSTS Horseshoe-shaped counters at which trading in assigned stocks takes place at the New York Stock Exchange. Specialists' order clerks and exchange employees stand inside the posts, while specialists and brokers negotiate their transactions outside the posts.

TUBE CLERK An employee of the New York Stock Exchange who relays messages and orders from brokers' booths around the perimeter of the floor to specialists' posts in the center through a pneumatic tube system. Limit orders and reports on execution of these orders are also sent through the system, whose tubes are buried under the floor of the Exchange building.

TWO-DOLLAR BROKER An independent New York Stock Exchange member on the floor who handles transactions for other brokers. The name is derived from the fee of two dollars for every one hundred shares executed that was charged many years ago. Today's fees are considerably higher.

BIBLIOGRAPHY

ALLEN, FREDERICK LEWIS. *The Great Pierpont Morgan.* New York: Harper, 1949.

BARRON, CLARENCE W. *They Told Barron.* New York: Harper, 1930.

BARUCH, BERNARD M. *Baruch: My Own Story.* New York: Henry Holt, 1957.

BROOKS, JOHN. *The Go-Go Years: When Prices Went Topless.* New York: Weybright and Talley, 1973.

——. *Once in Golconda.* New York: Harper & Row, 1969.

——. *The Seven Fat Years.* New York: Harper, 1958.

CLEWS, HENRY. *Fifty Years in Wall Street.* New York: Irving, 1908.

CORY, LEWIS. *The House of Morgan.* New York: AMS Press, 1969.

DIES, EDWARD. *Behind the Wall Street Curtain.* Washington, D.C.: Public Affairs Press, 1952.

DOUGLAS, WILLIAM O. *Democracy and Finance.* New Haven: Yale University Press, 1940.

FISHER, IRVING. *The Stock Market Crash—and After.* New York: Macmillan, 1930.

FULLER, JOHN G. *The Money Changers.* New York: Dial Press, 1962.

GRODINSKY, JULIUS. *Jay Gould: His Business Career, 1867–1892.* Philadelphia: University of Pennsylvania Press, 1957.

HOOVER, HERBERT. *The Memoirs of Herbert Hoover: The Great Depression, 1929–1941.* New York: Macmillan, 1952.

KELLOGG, JAMES C., III, and DOWNEY, WILLIAM E. *The Stock Market Crash of 1929.* Elizabeth, N.J.: J. C. Kellogg Foundation, 1954.

KEMPNER, S. MARSHALL. *Inside Wall Street: 1920–1942.* New York: Hastings House, 1973.

KLIMLEY, APRIL. *Here Is Your Career: Banking, Money and Finance.* New York: Putnam, 1978.

KREFETZ, GERALD, and MAROSSI, RUTH. *Money Makes Money.* New York: World, 1970.

LEFFLER, GEORGE L. *The Stock Market.* New York: Ronald Press, 1951.

MALKIEL, BURTON. *A Random Walk down Wall Street.* New York: Norton, 1973.

MARTIN, RALPH G., and STONE, MORTON D. *Money, Money, Money.* Chicago: Rand McNally, 1960.

MAYER, MARTIN. *New Breed on Wall Street.* New York: Macmillan, 1969.

——. *Wall Street: Men and Money.* New York: Harper, 1955.

MEEKER, J. EDWARD. *The Work of the Stock Exchange.* New York: Ronald Press, 1922.

NEY, RICHARD. *Making It in the Market.* New York: McGraw-Hill, 1975.

——. *The Wall Street Jungle.* New York: Grove Press, 1970.

PECORA, FERDINAND. *Wall Street Under Oath.* New York: Simon & Schuster, 1939.

REGAN, DONALD. *A View from the Street.* New York: New American Library, 1972.

RHEINSTEIN, SIDNEY. *Trade Whims.* New York: Ronald Press, 1960.

"SMITH, ADAM" (GOODMAN, GEORGE J.). *The Money Game.* New York: Random House, 1968.

SOBEL, ROBERT. *Inside Wall Street.* New York: Norton, 1977.

———. *NYSE: A History of the New York Stock Exchange, 1935–1975.* New York: Weybright and Talley, 1975.

———. *The Big Board: A History of the New York Stock Market.* New York: The Free Press, 1965.

SPARLING, EARL. *Mystery Men of Wall Street.* New York: Greenberg, 1930.

SWANBERG, W. A. *Jim Fisk: The Career of an Improbable Rascal.* New York: Scribner, 1959.

WEISSMAN, RUDOLPH L. *The New Wall Street.* New York, Harper, 1939.

WELLES, CHRIS. *The Last Days of the Club.* New York: Dutton, 1975.

WISE, T. A., and the editors of *Fortune. The Insiders: A Stockholder's Guide to Wall Street.* Garden City, N.Y.: Doubleday, 1962.

INDEX

Date Du